Voices of the Future

Voices of the Future

Presented by Etan Thomas

Haymarket Books
Chicago, Illinois

© 2012 Etan Thomas

Published by
Haymarket Books
P.O. Box 180165,
Chicago, IL 60618
773-583-7884
info@haymarketbooks.org
www.haymarketbooks.org

ISBN: 978-1-60846-271-1

Trade distribution:
In the US through Consortium Book Sales and Distribution, www.cbsd.com
In the UK, Turnaround Publisher Services, www.turnaround-uk.com
In Canada, Publishers Group Canada, www.pgcbooks.ca
In Australia, Palgrave Macmillan, www.palgravemacmillan.com.au
All other countries, Publishers Group Worldwide, www.pgw.com

Special discounts are available for bulk purchases by organizations
and institutions. Please contact Haymarket Books for more information
at 773-583-7884 or info@haymarketbooks.org.

Cover design by Eric Kerl.

This book was published with the generous support of the Wallace Global Fund
and Lannan Foundation.

Printed in Canada by union labor.

Library of Congress CIP Data is available.

1 3 5 7 9 10 8 6 4 2

Contents

Foreword by Chuck D

As a young single-digit-aged child in the 1960s, I grew accustomed to grown folk in my vicinity taking the lead and acting most of the time . . . like grown folk. There was a definite line between kids, teenagers, and adults. As many good times as I enjoyed as a child, I also knew that the time was very serious. Television kicked into second gear, radio was a cultural god voice. Reading was fun, fundamental and escapism into a world past, present and future. Books were a release as well. It was also a time when the athletes and entertainers of that day reflected the thoughts, ideals, goals, and dreams of the people from whence they came. They had to. Whether it was Dr. Martin Luther King Jr., Minister Malcolm X, or Judge Thurgood Marshall, the cheapest price for a grown person to pay at that time was attention. It still is. The black entertainers and athletes of that day had to be conscious. They reflected the climate and the attitudes of the people.

The name changes of Black athletes alone were jarring to my single-digit-aged self back in that day. That alone seemed to make up for the lack of microphone and TV time they were experiencing. You know, bad for the ratings. Let them be seen doing their ball thing, but definitely do not let them be heard. Many athletes in that era protested violations of civil rights. Many of them knew that they weren't speaking for themselves; they were standing tall for a constituency that was silenced by a society splitting at a bad seam. I read philosophical books by Black athletes as a child and teenager because I knew it was where many of us wished to be. We dreamed of those physical gifts we watched, but the goods was the sciences they dropped on us, not the ball.

The 70s and 80s, the silencing and the casting off of the black athlete, made many go for "delph" as the 1990s hip-hop Wu Tang slang depicted. The money got bigger because a baseball player named Curt Flood sacrificed his career to end the slavery system of the Reserve Clause. Black athletes figured that the best way to fly through an airport was to zip the lip and brain and get some mainstream fuel. Once they were freed as agents of commerce, the separation between the athlete and fan widened like the Gap Band. You would figure the complete disenfranchisement and chastisement of the Black community following the R & B years (that's Reagan and Bush) would make the last 30 years of Black athletes . . . say . . . something. Maybe not. Even physical statements such as Mahmoud Abdul Rauf's 1994 beliefs in prayer, peace not war and refusal to patronize a contradictory symbol of it, made the rest of the flock fly away. We know that the games have changed—more power, speed, and accuracy. But what has happened to the athletes' minds? Especially the ones of color, many of whom dare not make a peep about the politics of the country we reside in, much less the earth surrounding us.

Etan Thomas is the exception, and the deal is that this man does not want to be an exception. He wants to raise the perception of his sport, eradicate the stereotype of greed and shallowness. His word is even more of a power move than his 6-10 260 drive to the basket, block or rebound. His words are a powerful assist to mankind. He has seized to prism the rainbow of light that is beamed to the doorways of our athletes and entertainers, to the masses. Etan Thomas is not simply a throwback, nor is he a throwaway. He is a portal of our future in the brilliant words he speaks and writes. I am truly honored to introduce this man's poetic justice, a written presentation of true justice and the international way. He has challenged young people to voice their opinions. He has offered them an outlet to the world, used his position as a platform for others.

With so many young people today looking for things to happen, grasping for the air granted to athletes and entertainers when what they need is something that is mentally nourishing, life building, discover Mr. Etan Thomas delivering so necessary a book that it truly deserves the term *fantastic*.

Peace.

Introduction by Etan Thomas

Voices of the Future is a project that allows young people to express their opinions, beliefs, and thoughts to the world. The book is broken down into sections by subject matter. Each section begins with a selection from an interview I did with political sportswriter Dave Zirin, followed by a poem of mine and the writings of the young authors. And, just to be clear, I wasn't interested in getting a lot of young people who view a certain topic the same way I do. I wanted to get all opinions and beliefs, no matter what side of the fence these young people are on. I wanted them to speak with passion and present their position through poetry or prose.

This book also contains a CD insert with tracks of me reciting some of my poems to beats. I did this with my first book, *More Than an Athlete*, and it seemed to go over pretty well. Sometimes young people like to hear poems in addition to reading them, so it's good to have that option. I remember when I was younger listening to the works of poets like the Last Poets, Gil Scott Heron, and Shakespeare on CDs. Even now, listening to poets like Saul Williams, Black Ice, Talaam AC, Queen Sheba, or 13 of Nazareth, on CDs, just gives you a whole different feel for the poems.

I think that adults don't give young people enough credit. Adults think that young people are only interested in BET and MTV and video games, but that is far from true. That's why with this new book project I want to show the side of young people that often goes unheard. I wish people would be able to see what I see when I go and speak at some of these schools. These young people are up on current events; they know the issues, have well-expressed positions and present their arguments well. I remember one time going to a charter school in DC, and I asked the audience what they wanted to talk about. I do that sometimes because I would rather know what's on their minds than stand up there and talk their ears off for whatever time is allotted. Well, I asked this question and they wanted to talk about gay marriage. I looked at the teachers and they said it was fine with them. Then, the debate started. Hands started shooting up all over the audience, one after the other. These were teenagers expressing positions for gay marriage and against it.

Another time shortly after the DC Sniper John Muhammad was caught, I spoke at a school in Maryland and the students wanted to debate the death penalty. Their arguments were amazing. Some spoke from a spiritual standpoint, others from an emotional standpoint, others argued the difference in sentencing due to economics or quality of representation, others argued the need for a deterrent. All of their arguments stemmed from the fact that everyone in DC was terrified and shocked by the horrible acts of the DC Sniper.

They presented the same arguments you would hear on CNN or MSNBC. But adults for some reason don't believe that young people have opinions on these subjects. Even some of the teachers of the kids were a little hesitant with some topics that I wanted to include. But my manager, Carlisle Sealy, made a good point to me in saying that hopefully if this project goes well, we will do a volume 2, and we can explore even more topics that we didn't get to with this book. But overall, we have a good list of sections allowing for a wide variety of opinions and concerns of young people to be heard.

Some of the young people requested that their names be entered as anonymous. I wanted them to feel free to express themselves in any way they saw fit, but respected the fact that not all of them wanted their identity to be known. A lot of them told me, "Hey, you're in the position where you can say what you want and not have to worry about the consequences; some of us are saying things that could come back to haunt us." It's interesting, because I always heard people warn me to be careful what I said, but I respect their decision. I just asked that I could put their age so that the reader can see the dept of their thoughts and opinions at such a tender age.

I don't want anyone to think that my goal here is to financially profit from their work in any way shape or form. I am going to donate the proceeds to the Free Minds Book Club in Washington, DC, a great organization that is helping a lot of young people get their lives back on track emotionally, spiritually, and preparing them for postincarceration by giving them the tools that will enable them to be productive, outstanding members of society. But don't take my word for it, visit their website at freemindsbookclub.org and read their incredible success stories for yourself.

I think that everyone who reads this book is going to be impressed, just as I always am by the young people's writings. With this project, I want young people or anyone who reads this book to walk away with a few simple messages. Believe in yourself, stand up for what you believe in, overcome doubt, and never allow the haters to dictate your potential.

1.

President Obama

Pres. Obama must act upon his potential in order to become the great leader he has the capacity to become.
—John Jenkins

Dave Zirin: Let me ask you this, can you be critical of the President even though you support him?

Etan Thomas: Definitely, I think President Obama was holding on too much to a dream that the Republicans would ever work with him on anything. I think he wasted too much time with that. Even if they had a plan or initiative that they once were in favor of, how many times did we see that when that same plan came from President Obama, they were all of a sudden against it? They are not going to be on board with him, period. So enough wasting time trying to convince them to be reasonable. I know he still has to get the approval of Congress to do anything, but it just seems like he can take action in the ways the Constitution allows him to, like maybe use job creation, which this country desperately needs, using the military, and "I am going to dare you to try and stop me. You introduce your bills, you hold your hearings, you have your speeches; this is what I am going to do, so either you get on board or you stand to the side." I hate to say it, but that is how George W. Bush handled things. He went into Iraq even though he didn't have the approval of *anyone*. He made up a reason, lied about ties to 9-11; he knew there weren't any connections, but he was determined to push his agenda. Of course President Obama has more integrity than that, but what I am saying is, Bush didn't waste a lot of time trying to convince everyone. He just acted, and that is what I want to see President Obama do

Dave Zirin: Wow, you actually criticized a lot more than I thought you would. I have to say I am surprised to hear you say all of that. You kind of gave a compliment to George W. Bush.

Etan Thomas: No, I wasn't trying to give Dubya any compliment, but honestly the Republicans' entire objective is to make the President look bad so they can say "Look how bad the economy is, look how high the unemployment rate is," as they shoot down everything that he has done to try to help improve those conditions, and now the country will need the good ol' Republicans to swoop in the 2012 elections and save the country. Senate Minority Leader Mitch Mcconnell said that his top priority is defeating President Obama. So they are putting their personal feelings against the President above saving the economy, above protecting our shores; he puts that before the well-being of the citizens of the United States, which is the ultimate treason. And how could you expect to do a deal with someone who thinks like that? But I digress. What is your critique of President Obama's first four years?

Dave Zirin: The use of unmanned drones that have killed innocents abroad, the ordered "extrajudicial" killings, the declaring war in Libya without congressional approval—these are frightening powers to exercise. They aren't powers I trust Mitt Romney to have. They aren't powers I trust anyone to have. As for social policy, it's on us to build movements to fight for a changing policy toward immigrants, toward women, or toward the poor. No president does that for you without being pushed.

Etan Thomas: Well, what do you think of the alternative, Mitt Romney?

Dave Zirin: Mitt Romney is so out of touch, it's a joke. He's the ultimate 1%er. He is the personification of everything the Occupy movement was fighting against: corporate greed, profits before people, and a complete absence of scruples.

Etan Thomas: So you think there is a need for another option, like a third party?

Dave Zirin: I wish we could break the two-party duopoly and get more ideas up there in the debates and in the political oxygen of this country. How remarkable would it be if there was someone in the debates who was for legalizing marijuana, or closing down the US military bases overseas, or starting a federal jobs program? They might not win the election, but we'd all be better off if people had access to those ideas.

Etan Thomas: Okay, but there is a big difference between maybe having a legitimate argument that Pres. Obama could do more for the poor and Romney and Ryan, whose policies are obviously against the poor. Let's look at some facts.

Ryan is the chief architect for the Republican Party's plan for tax and spending cuts and an advocate of reshaping the country's Medicare program. The austere budget proposal that bears Ryan's name would cut $770 billion from Medicaid and other health programs for the poor over 10 years, as compared with President Obama's recent budget. He also takes an additional $205 billion from Medicare and an additional $1.6 trillion from food stamps, welfare, federal employee pensions, and support for farmers. In addition, his plans include changing Medicare into a program that would rely largely on vouchers.

To add insult to injury, Ryan's budget would offset these $5.3 trillion in spending cuts by offering a $4.2 trillion tax cut to the wealthiest in this country, according to Citizens for Tax Justice.

Whew. Looks like it will be a long winter for the 99 percent if the Wisconsin congressman gets his way. So if Romney and Ryan got in office and this plan were put in place, those who criticize President Obama for not doing enough for the poor and middle class would really be singing the blues, because it will be all downhill from there.

Dave Zirin: There is definitely a difference. But true programs that actually tackle poverty will only happen if we build a movement to make it happen. As Howard Zinn, the historian, said, what matters is not who's sitting in the White House. It's who's sitting in the streets.

On the CD you have an impassioned poem called "The Inauguration" where you describe what that day meant to you. To quote you, "Reaching heights of dreams deeply rooted in the minds of kings that weathered the storms from sea to shining sea." Take me through that entire feeling.

Etan Thomas: Well, in that line I am describing Dr. Martin Luther King's dream. And the "storms from sea to shining sea" is a reference to everything we as Black people have had to overcome in this country. My grandfather said it best on the CD, "We have come a million miles, you can call it a million but it's further than that." We have been through so much as a people in this country.

I have a poem in *More Than an Athlete* called "Don't Think I Forgot" that really takes you through our plight in this country. We have been through a lot and persevered.

Dave Zirin: I remember this poem. It was very moving, and hearing it on your CD really brought the emotion of it all to life.

Etan Thomas: Yea, it's a tough one for people to listen to. So for us to be able to reach this height of having President Barack Obama become the 44th president of the United States is something that I as a Black man take great pride in. Look at what we have had to overcome. What we had to endure. It's much deeper than just being happy to have a Black man in the Oval Office. Now, young people across the nation see as a possibility what you can become if you don't allow anyone or anything to stop you. They see that no amount of negative statistics, unfavorable situation, broken home, single-parent household, can keep you from achieving your goal. President Obama is a symbol of what is possible. Before, it didn't even seem a possibility. If someone were to say they wanted to be President of the United States, it would be some far-fetched dream like I want to go to the moon or walk on water. Now it is a possibility because the sky's the limit.

Four More Years
By Etan Thomas

"The road ahead will be long. Our climb will be steep. We may not get there in one
    year or even in one term. But, America, I have never been more hopeful
    than I am tonight that we will get there."
That was in 2008 and now in 2012 there is still so much to be done
Too many Americans are still with their lives firmly gripped around pain
They're like Linus where over their heads remains an ever existing cloud of rain
The time in their hourglass of hope has just about run out of sand
There is still despair in the Dust Bowl and depression across the land
Yes we can, even though the right has done everything in its power to leave us
    drowning in quicksand
Sending a memo to veto any bill written by the President's hand
We have an unbelievable percentage of Americans living in poverty and a de-
    plorable unemployment rate
But they want to vote down in unity any job creation or economic development plan
They would rather play political games so they can say how bad the economy remains
They wanna take you to a metaphorical hospital bed to lay your freedoms and
    liberties to rest
And instead of the morphine drip of tax breaks or health care for pain ease
They hydrate you with lies about Obamacare intravenously
Smoke and mirrors
To bring you clearer
To their side of the Tea Party
And have your dream of a pursuit of happiness float away like a feather in the wind
So they can then ride the waves
Of singing praise
Of "ding dong, the witch is dead"
But their wicked witch has the middle name Hussein instead
Fox News is like poison with adrenalin,
Slithering through your TV screen with their far from fair and balanced type
    sentiment
But even with the right wanting his head on a platter like a guillotine

The fact remains that he has managed to create more private-sector jobs in 2010
    alone than the entire Bush years had ever seen

Now, there are some who say that President Obama isn't doing enough for the poor

Or that he has ignored the issues of the community and doesn't even have a desire
    to do more

They say that he's closed the door on the country's impoverished working poor and
    middle-class core

That's simply not true

Now I'm not saying that President Obama should be exempt from criticism

He is not perfect

Nor am I suggesting that he has never made a decision that has ever been
    doubtable

Nor do I believe it is some act of racial treason for a Black person to hold our
    President accountable

The fact is there is still a lot that needs to be done to ensure that all Americans
    have the opportunity to soar

But with all due respect: if they think they have issues with the President not doing
    enough for the poor now, what do they think will happen if Mitt Romney
    takes office? Then they would really need a poverty tour.

Don't forget the mess he walked into

Bush had eight years to leave the economy in shambles

Tangled in a web of mismanagement

A crisis this deep didn't happen overnight

One of the biggest cleanup jobs in American history is what was laid at President
    Obama's feet after election night

But to date, he has created more than 4 million new jobs, our auto industry is back
    on top and American manufacturing is growing for the first time since
    the 1990s

He signed the Lilly Ledbetter Fair Pay Act, restoring basic protections against pay
    discrimination

Through the HIRE Act he massaged an ointment of an 18-billion-dollar tax break
    into the aching joints of small businesses without hesitation

He's focused on closing the gap between the prince and the pauper

He extended unemployment insurance, attempting to melt down a hard-knock life
    into something softer

A wise man once said that education is the key to success

But if that door is locked then you've stopped the possibility of that rose from the
concrete growing at its best

To be frank,

the right only cares about educating the kids of the 1 percent

So having brand-new metal detectors but old outdated books in inner-city schools
doesn't bother them one bit

But President Obama has already made historic progress:

Local schools are now empowered to raise their standards

The Student Aid and Financial Responsibility Act he signed

made repaying student loans a little easier to manage

He also expanded Pell Grants, which help low-income students pay for college

How could you even think of changing course when President Obama is in his
prime like Optimus

Through the Dream Act President Obama has shown the he understands a fact
that for some reason Republicans can't wrap their minds around

That immigrants are in integral part of our nation

And it was through immigrants that this nation was founded

He suspended the deportation of illegal immigrants under the age of 30 who came
to the US before age 16, and who have lived in the country for at least five
years.

They are eligible if they have no criminal records, are in school, or are high school
graduates

He has given young immigrants the chance at the American Dream if they handle
their business

Because no other law on the books punishes children for the crimes of their parents

His Health Care Reform Bill now prevents insurance companies from denying
people because of preexisting conditions

Not to mention that

it also allows children to remain covered by their parents' insurance until age of 26

So after they finish college and they're in that in-between time and they enter the
workforce and entry-level positions their health care can continue to exist

He also cut prescription drug costs for Medicare recipients by 50%

He supports women being able to have preventative care covered by health insur-
ance because as a human being having that right makes logical sense

Working families are now paying lower taxes

And the President cracked down on Wall Street recklessness and abuses by health
insurance, credit card and mortgage companies by making them raise
their standards
We need an economy that creates the jobs of the future and makes things the rest
of the world actually wants to buy
not one built on outsourcing, loopholes or risky financial deals that jeopardize
everyone's pie in the sky
basic fundamentals that Republicans could really care less about
See, they want you scrambling for crumbs like the Hunger Games for their enter-
tainment
Take away your access to health care and a quality education
Flip your rights like a spatula
While *they're* married to the fruits of the American Dream
They wanna keep stringing you along like a dedicated bachelor
Waving the possibility of a ring in front of your face like a man without character
Wasted motions running on a treadmil going nowhere but still
Stressing your cardiovascular
And tax you like you have no dependents
To stop and frisk your right to peacefully exist right out of existence
Our work is far from done.
We now stand at a make-or-break moment for the middle class, and America faces
a clear choice in this election:
I personally don't need a tax break
But teachers, firemen, construction workers, receptionists, farmers, Joe the
plumbers, those are the ones we need to help along
Trickle-down economics where only the 1 percent is granted the rights of liberty
and justice is just plain wrong
It's the right's never-ending story without the white flying dog
To go back in time like Marty McFly taking the Delorian in hopes of exploring the
previous failed Bush policies
Or we can move forward toward a nation built from the middle class out and
where everyone has the chance to succeed
On the path where all Americans will be able to earn enough to raise a family,
send their kids to school, own a home, put enough away to retire and
have enough food on their table to eat
President Obama wants to make sure that hard work actually pays off

And people are equipped with the proper tools
Where responsibility is rewarded, everyone has a fair shot, does their fair share
and plays by the same rules
That's what this election comes down to
Don't let them stop you from voting with their tricks of reducing the number of eligible voters,
Purging voting rolls, purposely giving misinformation about voting procedures
and voters needing a photo ID
Because all Americans regardless of race, color, religion, income, tax bracket, or
economic status deserve the right to truly be free

Inauguration
By Rocky Bright
25 years old

In the oval office, set a new precedence
Stained oak bedrooms named after past presidents

The press conference before brunch placed the media in remission
No questions asked, they honor the executive decisions

She loved him before he began to soar, that made him respect her more
Fresh flowers for the first lady flown in from Ecuador

Oil paintings of the Civil War smooth on the canvas
Where no [Black] man has ever gone, voyage to Atlantis

Sculpture in the foyer chiseled in bronze
Exquisite dining Maine lobster and prawns

No more tattered shoes, a new path discovered
Air Force One has Soul, far from rubber

Words soothe the masses, and keep them warm through the winter
Turned up the heat now the melting pot simmers

Chosen by the people, far from a token
Fluent in three languages but words are unspoken

His actions are watched with a bald eagle's precision
Spending cuts begin with minor incisions
The result of persistence, the need to acquire knowledge it
Educates the youth, place his daughters in private colleges

Foreign nations are aware, in hope they anticipate
Glory. The leader of the free world designate
Anger and resentment his opposition has
Please worry not for this too shall pass

Stability under pressure, his cabinet admires
Enter the war room and converse with top advisors

The parents no longer protest and picket
Sent the troops in the Middle East a one way ticket

No rest, shake every hand, remember every face
Found twenty minutes to doze on the staircase

Man of all men, daily sacrifice
For the purpose that the people will get a taste of paradise

A letter written to the mother of Obama, from the mother of Osama

By Kayla McAfee

16 years old

Have they come for your son yet?
It will be the morning
when the weight of your country
is brought to its knees

and you will see your son's face
for the first time.

We are the mothers of heavy hands.
You will think back to the day
you kissed the sunburn of war on his hands
and told him
"Protect your people."
The heartbeat of your nation
will be drowned out by the screams of children
and men.
You'll allow your hair to blow in the wind,
you'll realize how your life
is made of nothing but sand and blood.

. . . Have they found his hiding place yet?
Well, when they do, they'll dance and drink
till their hearts are contained.
The fires they'll start in the streets
will be their attempt at resurrecting
the lives he took.
His face will be forced in the minds of men
who only want to bring back their life
from ashes
to the kingdom they grew up with.

We are the mothers of kings.
You will think back
to how he raised his face to you and said
"Mommy, I'm going to change the world."
With the crushing of bone in his voice
and the burn of desert in his eyes,
he preaches.
He tells of how a majesty and power
only comes from the dust of broken people.
How art, mountains from the structure of dead bodies across the road.

The life is a privilege
and the necessity is trying to take it.
How music is raised from the heavens of gunfire.
Have you ever been sung to sleep
by the voices of bullets and the cracking of skulls?

No one asked me if I wanted my son to die.
No one asked me if I wanted my son to kill.
I was only shown
how my life
is made of nothing but sand and blood,
the morning the weight of my country
was brought to its knees
and I saw my son's face for the first time.

I kissed the hands
that frighten your country in its worst dreams.
I heard the crushing of bone in his voice,
and saw the burn of desert in his eyes.
I love him.
We are mothers.
Only wanting to push them back into our wombs
making them safe from the worlds they control.
War is our title.
And the heartbeats of our nations were and are
in the heavy hands of our kings.
Our sons.

If I Were Old Enough to Vote, President Obama Would Be My Choice as President
By Jaryd Jones

14 years old

As November 4th comes around the corner, it's a head-to-head matchup between this year's two candidates, and all eyes are on their next moves. For the Democratic Party, we have Barack Obama running again. As the incumbent, he hopes to win another 4 years in office. For the Republican Party, we have Mitt Romney, a Massachusetts governor that's well-known for his skill in finance. Though I may not be able to vote yet, I still have a good idea on who I would vote for in this year's elections. I would vote for the Democratic Party, because in my opinion, President Barack Obama is one of the most influential presidents of our time.

Even before he was elected, President Obama proved he could make an impact on the community most candidates never could. Before President Obama, I thought the title of president could only apply to white men, because that is all that was in office all these years. President Obama showed me that I too have the ability to do something as great as running a country. Following the Obama campaign also got me into politics. I learned how the elections truly worked after following the race between Obama and McCain. However, his influence did not just reach me. President Obama's appearance on the political field inspired millions of people. It empowered them with the thought that minorities do have a say in the government. I truly believe if President Obama weren't elected, no one would've had the motivation to protest like they do today. From Wall Street to the Trayvon Martin case, people marched and protested because they felt they could make a change. No one would've been able to do that if someone else was in charge. The Obama campaign really got people into politics. At first, the only thing people were voting for around this time was *American Idol* and *Dancing with the Stars*. In 2008, however, all voters, young and old, white and black, participated in the elections. I know for a fact that people from my neighborhood who've never cared about voting in their LIVES were seen in the line waiting for the ballot machine. Young voters became excited to vote, because they hoped they may have a chance to be heard. This is the impact our president has made on our community.

When President Obama is not running a country, he seems to be an excellent person to hang out with. He is a family man, always finding time for his loved ones. Besides, anyone that can juggle fame, a country, 3 females, AND a dog is cool with me. But in all seriousness, President Obama does not push his family behind him because he needs to run a country. He has learned to balance arguably the hardest lifestyle in the country. As a president, he takes his job with pride, and does not abuse his power, like some of our past presidents have. He also is very honest.

Finally, the last reason I respect President Obama is because even in the face of critics, he does not back down. He has the entire Congress currently trying to repeal his Obamacare. There are entire websites protesting about all that he has done. However, he stands strong. He doesn't let these and other troubles get in the way of his main goal: to get the country back on track. That is why President Obama is one of my biggest role models, and one of the most respected people in the world.

Despite President Obama's international influence, you'll notice he is having some trouble this year with the reelections. If you are a regular person looking at the reelection stats, you'd think President Obama would be burying Mr. Romney in a landslide right now, right? Not exactly what's happening right now? In fact if you look at the numbers so far, you'll see that the two candidates are actually neck and neck. However, according to political analyst David Brooks, President Obama should be "getting blown out of the water." No, Brooks is not a follower of the Nobama campaign or anything like that. He has his reasons to say what he said. According to his article in the *New York Times*, President Obama is lacking the four fundamentals needed to win a reelection. This list is based on how past presidents won reelection campaigns. First, your economy has to be in good shape. Already, President Obama is not doing too hot on the fundamentals. Second, most of the country has to like what you have done in your time as president (more or less obviously). President Obama has a pretty good stand on that, with his success with Obamacare. He also succeeded in helping clean up the BP oil spill, aiding Japan during the earthquake, and ending the war in Iraq. President Obama also signed economic stimulus legislation in the form of the American Recovery and Reinvestment Act of 2009 and the Tax Relief, Unemployment Insurance Reauthorization, and Job Creation Act of 2010. Other domestic policy initiatives include the Patient Protection and Affordable Care Act, the Dodd–Frank Wall Street Reform and Consumer Protection Act, the Don't Ask, Don't Tell Repeal Act of 2010, and the Budget Control Act of 2011. In May 2012, he became the first sitting US president to openly support legalizing same-sex marriage. In foreign policy, he ended the war in Iraq, increased troop levels in Afghanistan, signed the New START arms control treaty with Russia, ordered US involvement in the 2011 Libya military intervention, and ordered the military operation that resulted in the death of Osama bin Laden. He was also named the 2009 Nobel Peace Prize laureate. However, he still has had many critics. Based on a poll by ABC News, only 22% of voters believe that President Obama's take on a smaller government is a reason to vote for him. Also, the way he is governing isn't sitting well with some people. Some people believe he has governed from the left, but the country has somehow shifted to the right (David Brooks, *New York Times*). The third and final fundamental is gaining the votes of the neutral parties. President Obama has totally forgotten about winning the independent vote, and now cannot fall back on that when he needs to. Also according to recent Pew Poll studies, the percentage of Catholics supporting President Obama has dropped from 49% to 42. He has lost young voters as well. And on the same note, a recent study shows that the number of Hispanic voters has dropped by 5 percentage points.

By the way the stats are looking, it seems like President Obama should already be giving his office to Romney. So the question is, how is President Obama keeping an edge in this year's election? One reason is he has a much more unique background. Barack Hussein Obama is the 44th and current President of the United States. He is the first African American to hold the office. Born in Honolulu, Hawaii, he is a graduate of Columbia University and Harvard Law School, where he was the president of the *Harvard Law Review*. He was a community organizer in Chicago before earning his law degree. He worked as a civil rights attorney in Chicago and taught constitutional law at the University of Chicago Law School from 1992 to 2004. He served three terms representing the 13th District in the Illinois Senate from 1997 to 2004. The rest is history.

I'll be the first to admit that Mitt Romney has more experience in the financial field. This could help him in the election because the people want a president who can get us out of our current recession. However, people question his actual skill as a businessman. Though it is true that he saved 3 companies from going bankrupt, he did this by borrowing almost millions of dollars from the banks. So in a way, he put the companies in even MORE debt. This also makes people change their minds about voting for him. Another reason Barack has a lead is because he has created a better image for himself. If you ask a random person on the street what they think of Barack, they'll probably say something about he's a great guy, with a humble attitude and a big smile. When I asked a trusted individual (my teacher) about Mitt Romney, he stated, "I don't want that con man as a president!" Also, with the past stories of Romney bullying gay kids in high school, he's not looking too hot in the eyes of the public. The final reason President Obama might win is he has a level of charisma and empathy Romney will never have. When I talk about empathy, I mean the fact of the candidates knowing what the public is going through. President Obama has shown many times that he knows the feeling of what others are going through. When the earthquake hit Japan, he almost instantaneously sent packages of food, helpers, water, and clothing to assist them. He created Obamacare to help those who didn't have health care. Romney, he's not doing all that good on the empathy thing. As you know, Romney comes from the "high-class" end of the financial chart, so he's not too aware of how middle-class people live. One example of this is when he was speaking at the GM headquarters, where he says, "I am just like you. My wife owns 2 Chryslers, and I own 3 Cadillacs." This is exactly what I am talking about. Romney seems to have no idea that he is talking to the working class, who are lucky to even OWN a car themselves. Yet he claims to be just like them by owning FIVE of them. Another instance where he shows a lack of empathy is when he is speaking at a college in West Virginia, where he tells the students to "borrow money from your parents and start a business." Not a lot of kids have parents that can just strip money off of their clothes and give it to them. This is how Romney shows a lack of empathy, and this will hurt him in the upcoming elections.

In conclusion, if I were old enough to vote, President Obama would be my first choice as president. He not only is great at his job, but does it with pride. He also has an influence on the public that I do not believe Mitt Romney will never come near to. That is why Barack Obama would get my vote as president. My name is Jaryd Jones, the soon-to-be First President with a Super Bowl Ring, and I approve this message.

STAND
By Nya Wilson
10 years old

It's time to stand for the man
Who has led our land to understand
The importance of values
The importance of fairness
The importance of a helping hand.

President Obama made us see
That you and me could work hard and be
Anything we dreamed to be.

The 44th President of our county
No one knows where we would be
So it is a must that we all trust
The one who'll be there through good and bad
Happy and sad
So make a STAND for our 44th President of this land.

What President Obama Means to Me and If I Were Old Enough to Vote Would I Vote for Him?
By Nya Morgan
10 years old

When I think of President Obama I think of a man with lots of integrity. He is also a very kind and giving man. I learned about President Obama when he was a state senator in Chicago, Illinois, where I was born. I learned how when he was younger he helped citizens on the Southside of Chicago, where I lived. Throughout his life he worked hard in college and law school, even before he knew he would be president. He has shown me and other younger people that we should always do our best in school, work hard and be a good person because we never know what may be in store for our lives. He has also shown me that I should never limit myself because anything is possible.

I like that President Obama is always trying to figure out things and solve problems that can help improve this country. I also admire him because he never lets the bad things that are said about him get inside his head.

If I were old enough to vote I would vote for President Obama because I think that he has many more good ideas that could improve our nation, and he has made this country a better place.

President Obama's Potential
By John Jenkins
14 years old

Many people may suggest that President Obama has failed to meet the needs of our country. However, I am one that sees the potential Pres. Obama has to create change and push our country towards recovery. Potential is great to have, but potential means nothing without action. In order for Pres. Obama to put our country in a position where recovery is possible there are a few things he must do. First, Pres. Obama needs to separate the investment banks from the commercial banks. Also for economic growth Obama needs to rethink our budget, because we spend too much money on things like military defense rather than in struggling areas such as education. Lastly, Pres. Obama needs to learn to veto and repeal unconstitutional bills.

Our country is facing a devastating economic collapse. In order for the United States to see economic growth, Pres. Obama needs to reinstate the Glass-Steagall Act of 1933 to separate the commercial banks that serve consumers and businesses from the speculative investment banks. The Glass-Steagall Act is so critical because it helped repair our economy after the Great Depression. The Glass-Steagall would separate the corrupt investment bankers and corporations that push plutocratic standards upon our people. It is important to separate the investment bankers from commercial ones to investigate and monitor the investment banks that in the past have committed massive fraud in blowing up the housing bubble, entrapped unwary borrowers in mortgages that would explode, sold trillions of dollars worth of derivative contracts, and got the government to bail them out on worthless assets at face value (when they should have gone bankrupt or settled for 15–30 cents on the dollar). If Pres. Obama can reinstate the Glass-Steagall Act or pass an updated version of the act, he can put our economy in a position where recovery is within reach.

The United States does not focus enough on the vital areas that are needed. The United States has been trying the same thing in its budgets for years and expecting different results. That's a symptom of insanity. Pres. Obama has done well to re-evaluate the budget, but there is still much room for improvement. He has created the Bowles-Simpson Commission to recommend steps that could be taken to reduce future budget deficits. The commission released its report in November 2010, which recommended deep domestic and military spending cuts, reforming the tax system by eliminating many tax breaks in return for lower overall rates, and reducing benefits for Social Security and Medicare. The plan did not receive supermajority vote and was rejected before being brought to Congress.

The last thing Pres. Obama should consider is vetoing and repealing unconstitutional bills. Obama recently signed two very unconstitutional bills, the NDAA and HR 347. The NDAA gives the president dictatorial power in the name of "homeland security." What that means is it will allow the current president to implement martial law in times of war. In vague language, the HR 347 allows the government to arrest anyone who protests anywhere that an official has been. This is a violation of Americans' First Amendment right to protest. Pres. Obama should also attempt to repeal unconstitutional bills that are in effect now, such as the Patriot Act, which contradicts the Fourth Amendment. Pres. Obama must protect the rights of the people and defend us from attacks on civil liberties.

Pres. Obama must act upon his potential in order to become the great leader he has the capacity to become. If Pres. Obama can pass an updated version of the Glass-Steagall and rethink the budget, he can put our country in place to prevent another depression and repair our economy. In addition, he must protect the people from oppressing laws that violate our Constitution.

"Greatness is more than potential. It is the execution of that potential. Beyond the reach of talent." – Eric A. Burns.

President Obama Is an Inspiration to Us All
By Gloria Wiggs

19 years old

Do you remember in your early childhood being asked by an adult, "What do you want to be when you grow up?" Out of all the millions of children born in the United States every year, I am positive more than a few of them replied, "I want to be the president of the United States." Children from different racial backgrounds and raised in different societies share one common dream that Pres. Barack Obama made into a reality.

President Barack Obama is the 44th president of the United States. He has shown not only minority Americans but all Americans that if you believe in yourself you can succeed. He is a proven great leader, father and husband. President Obama took the role of cleaning up the mess that Pres. Bush made and stimulated change in our government. When most political officials were busy trying to make the rich richer, Pres. Obama has consistently worked to stimulate our economy and create jobs for middle- and lower-class citizens. He has never stopped his efforts to increase health care, make college more affordable, and help stimulate our economic growth.

There are many families that are grateful to President Obama. I am personally thankful for his work with financial aid, which had a direct effect on my life as a college student. There are communities filled with young adults who have opportunities they wouldn't possess if it had not been for him. I am grateful that his wife, First Lady Michelle Obama, has stepped forward with him, supporting all of his work and efforts for change.

From today forward children from different racial backgrounds will see President Barack Obama and be able to say, "I can be the president of the United States." They will have opportunities and privileges that without President Obama they might have had to do without. So, in this upcoming presidential election he has my vote, and I will always support President Barack Obama.

In 2012 My Vote Goes to President Obama
By William "Tippa" Thomas

25 years old

How many other presidents had their citizenship put into question? How many other presidents have had several efforts stalled and delayed with the clear intent of derailing their agenda because of their race? How many other presidents have had public displays of blatant racism against them?

How easily most forget that it took Bush eight years to drive the United States economy into a huge deficit, but we expect President Obama to rectify it in just four years.

Why has the GOP been so reluctant to pass legislation that will help turn the economy around? Is it because they don't want President Obama to be able to have any success and use that to garner support for reelection in 2012?

President Obama is the first president of the United States to publicly express his personal, not political, support of gay marriage. Obama is arguably the biggest figure of civil rights equality since the thrust of the civil rights movement. Yet he is criticized for his personal belief in another minority's pursuit of equality in society. The civil rights movement is incomparable to the gay rights movement, but the fight for equality amongst all human being is the same.

Most presidents have had two terms in office, and I believe he deserves another term to help rectify the damage that former presidents did. Under President Clinton, the United States economy was flourishing for eight years; however, Bush had the same economy in disarray in eight years. Obama should be allowed to finish his efforts to restore the economy to pre-Bush status.

In the past four years President Obama has been scrutinized tremendously, but most seem to forget all the good he has done for the economy despite the blatant resistance from the Republican Party. From the assassination of Osama bin Laden and ending the active organization of terrorist groups, to bringing the troops home from war, to making college more affordable, to unemployment extensions; he has done a phenomenal job.

When Obama took office, the economy was losing roughly 800,000 jobs a month. Facing these staggering numbers, he took proactive measures in the first few months of his term to stop the excessive job loss and to stop middle-class families from dropping into poverty. He also pushed for health care reform so low-income families could be able to afford basic health needs.

In my humble opinion, President Obama has not been perfect, but given the circumstances he faced when he took the presidential oath in 2008, and the consistent rebellion by Republicans, he is doing the best he can to restore America to the most powerful country in the world, which is why he will receive my vote in November 2012.

Our President

By Joe Rosga

15 years old

Bold, he is always one to take risks and or chances to help the people of his country.

Attitude, his attitude about something is what will drive him, and most of
the time it's for positive reasons.

Respect, the President respects all organizations, regardless of their history or
relationships.

Ambitious, Mr. Obama has always shown a desire to succeed and solve
whatever issue may come his way.

Confidence is what he has, and also what he has inspired in other people.

Keen, whenever I seem him on TV, he always seems to be showing enthusiasm
toward something or someone.

Obedient describes the way in which is he willing to comply with orders
and listen to others' laws.

Bravery, he is always ready for what is to come next, and takes it on with
courage and the strength needed to overcome whatever situation it may be.

Attentive, he is always one to pay close attention to the problems he is faced with
every day.

Meticulous, Mr. Obama always pays great attention to whatever
task is at hand and is also very careful and precise with his decision making.

Active, I feel like he is very involved in the community and wants to do as
much he can with the people just to gain their friendship and utmost respect.

2.
Trayvon Martin

Do you really think this country is post racial, when we are constantly reminded of our color, the reminder is not my issue, it's the reminder of the many that don't remember, it's the majority that think the only terrorism this country has seen was on the 11th of September
— Malik Moten

Dave Zirin: The Trayvon Martin case has taken the attention of the entire country. Tell me how it personally affected you.

Etan Thomas: When I heard about this case I immediately thought about my son Malcolm. That could have been anyone's son. The entire situation was just tragic and disturbing.

Dave Zirin: There are so many questions surrounding this case. We could create an entire book just on this case. What are some of your biggest questions with this case?

Etan Thomas: Well, Dave, you tell me if a Black man appointed himself captain of his neighborhood watch group and said he saw a suspicious-looking white man and ended up shooting and killing him, would he be in jail right now?

Dave Zirin: Yes, he would.

Etan Thomas: Stereotypes in clothing are something that has always existed. It used to be baggy clothes, stocking caps, hats turned backward, whatever the style was. Why doesn't Geraldo Rivera and those who think like him understand that it's not the hoodie, it's who is under the hoodie that is the issue? Does he understand that whether Trayvon had on a hoodie or a cowboy hat, George Zimmerman was going to look at him as a threat?

Dave Zirin: Very true.

Etan Thomas: Am I being too pessimistic in being concerned that even with all of the evidence George Zimmerman may still get off for this killing? I am troubled at the thought of the tremendous blow it would be to the hearts and minds of people all across

America, people who have taken up this cause and who have been personally affected and tormented as more facts are discovered. What happens if justice doesn't prevail?

This takes me back to middle school when I heard the infamous Rodney King verdict. Over and over we saw the tape of Rodney King being beaten, just as we hear the tape of Trayvon Martin over and over. We hear George Zimmerman pursuing him, being told by the 911 dispatcher that they didn't need him to do that, and the rest of the facts being rolled out. I hear the New Black Panthers issue a bounty on the capture of George Zimmerman. With everything as intense as it is right now, what will happen if the final verdict for George Zimmerman turns out to be not guilty?

Trayvon Martin Case
Presents an Unfortunate Reality
By Etan Thomas

What do I tell my son
He's 5 years old and he's still thinking cops are cool
How do I break the news that when he gets some size
He'll be perceived as a threat and see the fear in their eyes
—Talib Kweli

My son Malcolm is six years old. He is a fun-loving kid, loves sports, *Avatar, The Last Airbender,* and swimming. Everyone thinks he is adorable. They look at his long dreadlocks, his big smile, his kind and playful heart, they comment on how respectfully he speaks to adults. He is a big kid—I am 6'10" and my wife is 6'0", so he's head and shoulders above everyone in his class. But soon, I have to explain to him that he will not always be viewed as a cute little kid. That as he gets older, that tall for his age, charming little kid with long dreadlocks will be looked at as a threat. He has an innocence that I am going to have to ruin for him very shortly. He is still under the impression that everyone will be treated fairly.

The case of Trayvon Martin is disturbing on so many levels I don't know where to begin.

According to published reports, on February 26th, Trayvon had gone to 7-11 during halftime of the NBA all-star game. He was walking back through a gated community where he was visiting a member of the community. George Zimmerman, who is not a member of any police force but rather a neighborhood watch captain, called 911 to report "a suspicious person" in the neighborhood.

Zimmerman: "Hey we've had some break ins in my neighborhood and there's a real suspicious guy at {address redacted}. This guy looks like he's up to no good or he's on drugs or something . . .") He later informed the dispatcher that that he looks Black. He then says, "He's staring at me."

While on the phone with the dispatcher Zimmerman is heard saying that Martin is "running." When asked where he replies "entrance to the neighborhood." You can hear deep breathing as the dispatcher asks Zimmerman, "Are you following him?" Zimmerman replies "yeah" and the dispatcher clearly says, "We don't need you to do that."

From this tape it sounds as if Trayvon was the one who was scared, which would be understandable if anyone turned around and saw a man looking at you in an SUV in the dark for no apparent reason. I would have been a little uneasy myself.

When police arrived, seventeen-year-old Trayvon Martin, who had a squeaky-clean record, no priors, and only a bag of Skittles, an iced tea, his cell phone, and his headphones, was dead from a gunshot wound admittedly by neighborhood watch captain George Zimmerman.

Zimmerman wasn't arrested because the police claimed to not have probable cause and Zimmerman claimed self-defense.

My question is, what exactly constituted self-defense?

An unfortunate reality is that in Zimmerman's mind, he didn't have to see a gun or actually see Trayvon doing something wrong. All he saw was that he was Black, as he repeated two times in the short 911 call. Is the unfortunate reality that young Black male = threat? Or does a young Black male at night = even more of a threat?

I'm not going to stress the fact that the National Crime Prevention Council that sets out the guidelines for how you run a neighborhood watch has a primary rule of thumb that you are not supposed to be armed.

Nor am I going to focus on the fact that since January of last year, Zimmermann has called police 46 times, or that in 2005 he was charged with resisting arrest and battery of a police officer and that alone should make him questionable as a neighborhood watch captain.

Nor am I going to argue that the Florida "Stand Your Ground" law ("A person who is not engaged in an unlawful activity and who is attacked in any place where he or she has a right to be has no duty to retreat and has the right to stand his or her ground and meet force with force, including deadly force if he or she reasonably believes it is necessary to do so to prevent death or great bodily harm to himself or herself or another or to prevent the commission of a forcible felony") couldn't be applicable in this case for the simple fact that as heard from the released tapes, Zimmermann left his vehicle and went after Trayvon.

Nor am I going to make the race of Zimmermann the issue.

To quote Rev. Al Sharpton:

> The race/ethnicity of Zimmerman or any citizen in this type of scenario doesn't matter, because at the end of the day, it is the race of the victim—Trayvon—that does matter. It is his race and his demographic that is consistently depicted as the threat, and negatively portrayed in popular culture.

It is this perception that I have to teach my son very soon. The unfortunate reality is that in Zimmerman's mind, he was justified and understandably afraid as soon as he laid eyes on young Trayvon. He didn't see a cute little kid who was drinking an iced tea. He saw a threat, a criminal, someone who could be on drugs or "up to no good."

Very soon I have to ruin my son's rose-colored-glasses view of the world we live in.

I have to teach him several things:

1. There are going to be people who view you as the enemy when you have done nothing wrong.

2. You are going to be feared, suspected, harassed, accused, and some people will be terrified of you.

3. If the police stop you, make sure you stop in a well-lit area and don't make any sudden moves. Keep your hands visible. Avoid putting them in your pockets.

4. Orally broadcast your actions (for example, "Officer, I am now reaching into my pocket for my license").

5. Always get the receipt after making a purchase, no matter how small, so no one can falsely accuse you of theft later.

6. I have to teach him about Emmett Till, James Byrd Jr., Amadou Diallo, Sean Bell, Oscar Grant, Timothy Stansbury Jr., Danroy Henry, Ramarley Graham, Kendrec McDade, Patrick Dorismond, and Johnny Gammage, who were all unarmed at the time they were killed.

7. Many times you're going to be viewed as guilty even when you're innocent.

I have to teach him these things for his own safety. I wish I didn't have to take away his innocence, but for his own well-being soon I will have to.

What Do You See?
Questions from Trayvon Martin to His Killer
By Jonathan B. Tucker

27 years old

What do you see when you look at me?
You don't look me in the eyes
So what is it you're looking for?
Am I the kid who beat up your brother in middle school?
Am I the one who stole his bike and you couldn't do anything about it?
Do you see vengeance in me?
A chance to get back at him? To get over?
To "make things right"?

Is that why you followed me?

Or are you a "teacher"? A righteous educator taking life lessons to the street
With a bully curriculum and a 9mm?
Do I look stupid to you?
What was your GPA?
Do I look like I need to learn a lesson
Hard as steel today?

Aren't we all stupid to you?
Aren't we all carrying guns and breaking laws?
Or is that just you?

Really, what do you see?
What can you see?
Can you see my father? Or does my skin preclude me from having great male role
      models like yourself?

I hear you mentor black boys; what have you told them
About hoodies and iced tea?

What of Jim Crow and self-defense laws?
What of segregation and privilege?

Have you shown them what streets they cannot walk?
What white ladies they cannot talk to
Or whistle at
In this sundown town?

Have you drawn chalk outlines for them
To step into for the "safety of the community"?
Have you told them how much their hair reminds you of drugs,
Their noses violence, their lips rape, their skin crime?
Have you scared them into forgetting their pride
And cowering before you, Massa?

Or are they just the exceptions to your black rules?
Just the Oprahs and Obamas among the 99% of us thugs?

Am I all hoodies and jeans to you?
All crack and rap and basketball?
Am I not a child still?

Can you not see my mother in my cheeks?
Her joy and laughter and pain and hope
Breathing through my lungs?
Is she not holy, not sanctified, not deserving?
Like your mother?
Can you see her grief?

Can you touch one-tenth of the earthquake
Rumbling in her chest every morning she wakes
Without me?
Can you imagine the almighty strength she wields
To prevent herself and my father from finding
Sweet relief in the same violence turned around?

Can you see how God she is?
How God we all are?
Even you?

I wonder, truly
What do you see?
What can you see
In me
Besides bullets?

I Wonder
By Brandon Douglas
20 years old

I see all of the news reports
All of the newspaper magazine and Internet articles
Facebook statuses and events
All of the Twitter hash tags
And I can't help but wonder if they'd do the same for me,

What if it was me,
What if I lost a fistfight to a gun hugged too tightly by its owners,
Would the heat of racial profiling and prejudice from that barrel rock an entire
        nation enough to protest violence and injustice once again?
I wonder if there would be fist pumps
Repetitive chants
And picket signs in my honor.
Would they mail empty cans of Sprite
Or empty boxes of Lemonheads
To my killer?

I wonder how he would feel knowing that the backlash is coming b/c he shot a
        young black man down,
I wonder if they would write him letters
fueled with hatred

And passion
And rebellion
And all of the other mess that's boiling inside,
Hearts heavy with pain
Scribbling poems of anger,
Holding on to a higher foundation
Like hangers.
The dangers are obvious,
They are what I am up against
Every single day of my life.
Just because I was born with a skin tone similar to Earth itself
Doesn't mean I should be treated like dirt.

I wonder if my feelings would matter to anybody.
Would I become the hash tag of the moment?
Will people express their appreciation for a group of words put together in my
        honor
With a simple thumbs up from afar?
I wonder if anybody would care enough to actually pursue justice
Instead of just praising the idea of it.
Us human folk
Have a tendency to crush the possibility of change under the weight of bad life
        experiences.
Hope doesn't seem to be as plentiful as it used to be where I come from.

It doesn't get a lot of coverage
And it's because that "isn't what the people need to hear."

Which leads me to wonder if the media would attempt a full court press on my
        mother's privacy,
I wonder how she would feel knowing that she is famous by association
With the victim of a crime,
I wonder if she would realize that the high-profile investigation being conducted is
        saturated in filth,
Serving as a distraction
From the heart of the situation,

A child was murdered.
The semantics shouldn't matter,
But unfortunately they do,
Who
When
Where and
Why
Always makes a difference,
The focus is usually on everything except for what it is.
It's messed up
Like sexism
Oppression
Racism
Violence,
The things that drive us apart and pit us against each other.
Who really wants to face these things?
When will we come together to fight to the death against all the things that hurt us?
Where will we go if things stay the way they are?
Why do people have die in senseless manners in order to bring attention to social
        injustices?

I just hope that something will happen
That can bring about a kind of understanding strong enough to influence change,
So I won't have wonder as much.

Outside Looking In
By Aleeyah Hampton
16 years old

Boom! Dead within a instant
Bullet from a pistol hole in the head
Skin that's been bled
From a struggle of a man
Who weighs heavier than the kid himself

A story too many details that's been told repeatedly
I can tell by the spread of the news a chaotic catastrophe
All of last memory was him screaming for help
Phone hung up girlfriend was struck
In the past convo told him to run and he tried
Zimmerman the zimmer was faster
No Dr. Seuss just that Tray was the itsy bitsy spider
Zimmer had this crazy idea that he was the exterminator
Illusion . . . why can't this all be an illusion
To father, mother and the brother
When right before he came from a store
No vodka just walking with an Arizona and 1 pack of Skittles
So this is not a funny issue especially to my black people
Tired of racism and stereotyping
We refuse to have these situations on replay
I'm just a citizen mixing the given into a story as if I'm a DJ
This world has been wearing hoodies in the past few weeks
For we will be his defense as well as jury
So Tray rest in peace
Zimmer coming up next justice before or after
Check it out worldwide search black panther
Called the man in blue about suspicion from a boy who gave you a broken nose
Just funny how he's dead and you're not injured
Great job Pinocchio now the Martin family has a lost
Hey I don't know the whole story just the given facts
Flashlight on the hip gun on the waist
Told you to calm down and stay in your place
I'm on the outside looking in and it doesn't look good
Black on black crimes would have been locked up no question
So wrong how a white Puerto Rican and this crime have no connection
Sympathy to the Martin family as well as all who knew
I'm sorry Trayvon this happened to you like that
All would've been avoided if he listened to the man in blue
Hold up and stand back

The Blinder

By Malik Moten

18 years old

Do you really think this country is post racial, when we are constantly reminded of our color, the reminder is not my issue, it's the reminder of the many that don't remember, it's the majority that think the only terrorism this country has seen was on the 11th of September, we parade around as slaves with a mental and physical blockade of dilemma. Or more so diaspora. Have the children of the sun no soul? Have the children of the sun no goals? You are a fool to think Obama means blacks made it, election time is only used as a blindfold . . . I turn on the TV, and I see Jim Crow dance on BET, I see blacks searching for acceptance on MTV, I see the pastor's televised sermon in the style of Zip Coon. I see pale faces in Africa acting as help, I see commercials that portray black women as hating themselves. Day to day I'm surrounded by blacks in mental slumber waiting on movie and show premieres, avoiding their fears, avoiding their identity. How can you possibly think the same people that enslaved you are now here to help you? How can you think that anything they instill in you has any validity? You sit quietly in suspense waiting for master to wake you up, he will never give you a nudge or a pinch to tell you that you're American dreaming. The minute a African is born here the devils begin scheming . . . we own this planet and still pay rent, as intelligent as we are we have been bamboozled by Willie Lynch, my sisters and brothers are living in the fear of being lynched, because the density of our higher senses has been drenched with ignorance. You stand and put your hand over your chest for the national anthem, is this not the nation that blatantly murders us at will, is this not the nation that introduced drugs to our sub-par neighborhoods so we could deal, is this not a nation that teaches none realities and laughs at the fools that think they are keeping it real? How real are you? You would sell your soul for material wishes, with the government as your genie lamp, you are not innovative or creative, you are another pawn in their chess game, and we now self-induce the pain, we embrace the slave names that we were named, and you're waiting for master to tell you it is time for change. Am I deranged or suspicious, am I a statistic, will I be dead by a set age, or locked away in a cage? You take deep breaths and really think this is life, when they have learned to enslave you with no chains.

I pull the trigger as a bullet travels through the head of Trayvon Martin leaving him in cold blood lying on his chest, but in this situation Trayvon is white, now tell me, will I be under arrest? If you answer with yes then you must know how blatantly the laws that govern this country are based off of chaos and nonsense. There would be no need for protest, I would be behind bars and facing the death penalty with a manslaughter charge. I would not have even been able to walk to the police and tell them this white Trayvon looked suspicious and intended to do harm. There would be no "Well, it's possible, and maybe this and that"—it would not have carried on. Wake up, can you not see that no regard is held for your divine souls? They don't show their hatred from what they tell, but more so from what they withhold. They teach you that you are inferior because they well know your capacity is 9 ether. They teach you to ignore and deny the facts to no end so it is easier to take a people with no beginning or end and give them a beginning at slavery and slavery as their end. They teach you perfection is impossible so you would never think it's possible to live without sin. They teach you to look to skies, search outside of yourself because they know your power is within. They teach you these things because of their lack of a conscience and lack of soul with spitefulness towards you because you are blessed with the ability to ascend. We search everywhere but our soul for a source of power, we watch the clock when every second, minute, and hour, is ours. Media will do anything to destroy the image of anyone that is trying to make a real difference, the courthouse drinks wine and laughs as you march and protest because they know either way it goes down they will use white supremacy as their key witness. I do not blame white America; Black America, I find you guilty of tribal treason . . . Trayvon Martin happened, Troy Davis happened, Dr. York happened. So many other brothers were attacked and trapped but we are more concerned with things of no importance, the youth bows to Phil Knight's Foamposites and Michael's new Jordans. When only the awakening of your souls as a majority will bring the world's systems to order.

Trayvon Martin Could Be Me
By Jazz Thompson
11 years old

I am NOT Trayvon but I know many
Uncles, cousins, friends so many
Free to walk Our Father's streets
Wearing a hoodie eating Skittle treats
Drink a tea still ice cold
Pop-pop! gunned down only 17 years old
I am NOT Trayvon but could be me

My ground I'd stand, tender asking what you see
I would not think that when I wake
It'd be my last day to dream or step to take
White privilege profiling, not your job
The nerve to justify, our future you rob

3.

The Occupy Wall Street Movement

This is for everyone that walks the parameters of 15th and K Street
like they're looking at the primate house at the zoo.
Half laughing half pitying them for poppy-eyed idealism
—Olivia Weltz

Dave Zirin: I am sure many people have and will continue to ask you this question, why are you concerned at all about the Occupy Wall Street movement?

Etan Thomas: I have been asked this question a lot. How could someone who is wealthy be interested in a problem that doesn't concern him? The answer is simple: Because I wasn't always in this position. I haven't forgotten where I come from.

It's like that old story of the person who gets on the train and says, "OK, conductor, I am on—we can go now," and the conductor looks out his window and says, "What about all of the other people who are trying to get on?" and the man says, "I am not worried about them. I am on, so they are not my concern." That is just not the way I was raised to think.

Dave Zirin: Yeah, but you have to understand why some would be offended by you standing for something that isn't your issue.

Etan Thomas: Michael Moore explained to critics that just because he's wealthy doesn't mean he can't stand with those angry with America's economic system. He made this analogy when he was being criticized in a similar way . . . "'How can you claim to be for the poor when you are the opposite of poor?'" It's the same way that an all-male Congress voted to give women the vote, or scores of white people marched with Martin Luther Ling, Jr. . . . It is precisely this disconnect that prevents Republicans from understanding why anyone would give of their time or money to help out those less fortunate." I couldn't have said it any better.

Dave Zirin: So tell me, what exactly is the Occupy Wall Street movement to you?

What do you see them fighting for?

Etan Thomas: I have great admiration and respect for the Occupy Wall Street movements. The courage of those men and women and children to take a stand and say "Enough is enough" is admirable. OWS has people of different races, genders, religions, and political persuasions. They banded together to fight a common problem which was labeled as the "greed and corruption of the 1%." Their goal is to create a movement that empowers, in a nonviolent way, every man, woman and child who feels powerless.

The Ninety-Nine
By Julian Thomas
30 Years Old

So
I just stepped out of a secondary
role in a 1st rate stage production
Of Mice and Men, and I sat down on
the metro north rail and I,

well,
I got all inspired from reading an
excerpt from Ginsberg's "Howl"
with the rhythm of the words and the
call of the wild and the
old school landscape scene.

So I got all inspired from reading "Howl"
and I reached for my pad
no, my pad and my pencil,
no l.e.d. light needed or
battery-draining, annoying apps to be seen.

So I reached down for my pad
just to be disappointed
once again by the thoughts it charted
and the pain it gleamed.

Is this the America we changed for?
The world of our shadowy dreams?

We who have dared to tread the murky waters of
musing back-alley open mics and rundown theatre spaces,
The wayward unkempt hopes of
greyhound weary runaways
with dime and a dollar dreams.

We,
artisans of the underground with our beat box demos and
lazy ramen noodle nights. What do we do it for?
Is it really all about the benjamin payoff
and one simple moment of applause? The stopwatch
time span of the hot white lights in our eyes
and a possible standing O?

Those things are nice.

But no,
we do it for the comrades.
We do it for those late-night rehearsals
and weary empty stomach backstage
moments, with their dank musty
comfort and their blue-lit haze.

We do it for the secondhand therapy sessions on
dusty antique couches, for the cold hard jokes
with their bittersweet self-deprecating laughter
and their beer-soaked, knowing grins.

Those of us lucky enough to ride late
night trains to small damp basements
know what I'm talking about. And if
you don't, these words are poor reflection.

This is the America I fight for.

The unchained melody of the proletariat,
with its whirlwind of pain and ecstasy
and rat-raced, lucid madness.

We are the Ninety Nine

This is our country

This is our song

We work 9 to 5s and 10 to 6s on steamy
soup-drenched dishwashers and
haggle with line chefs in hell's kitchen over
a better price on a nickel bag of funk.

We serve highbrows with low morals
and smile through criticism, as they send
back their overcooked rib-eyes and luke
warm soup.

We are your central park
baby stroller warriors, treading a path
through your child's stiffly somber mental
development.

We who are raising your
toddlers and softly inspiring your tweens
with a gentle word and just the
right book recommendation.

Who put out fires on snowy midnight
first alerts, and answer cries of help
from wobbly EMT trucks,

Who build sturdier bridges on less
sturdy pay scales, and fix the potholed
streets of every metropolitan coast to
coast.

We don't want a free ride

All we want is our fair share

But we will fight if we have to

We will fight if we must

◆ ◆ ◆

We who work the dusty trails from
Portlandia to Baltimore, from Tallahassee to
Tucumcari, and every truck stop and Route 66
mom and pop motel between.

We will fight for this once sacred land
before it is finally taxed and taken away.

We will fight for our chance to survive the
onslaught of Orwellian surveillance
and over taxed, uninsured, non-representation.

We will fight

And fight we will.

But you,

All you brooks brother's phonies
and stock market croonies,

you fear mongering, hate peddling, 401K
squirreling, third generation,
trust fund inherited
wall street
corporate goons,

The only question is,

Will you

The Occupier
By Eric Powell aka E.L.P.J. (Aswad Fahd)
14 years old

Why do I occupy?
Because when I look into my mother's eyes, just before she cries,
I see a pyramid lie at the bottom of her iris . . .
And not the type made by my ancestors, Horus, Isis & Osiris; no . . .
From this, I get a different feeling; a sense of . . .
Unfair competition, self-centered individualism,
Loss of true vision, racism & lynchings . . .
I see at the bottom of this building, men, women & children,
Holding it up like it's the only reason that they're living,
Amongst them, I see things my mother suffers through every day,
Check to check wage, debt and bills to pay,
And an array of even worse ways that humans have to live in and stay,
They work for all and feed all . . .
Above them, I see people toastin', boastin', having a ball,
They seem to have esteem and no flaws, fancy cars, broads,
And to those below them, they call, and say,
"We eat for y'all!"
Why do I occupy?
Because when I look into my father's eyes, just before he cries,
I see a pyramid lie at the bottom of his iris . . .
And not the type made by my ancestors, Horus, Isis & Osiris; no . . .

From this, I get a different feeling; a sense of . . .

Unfair court decisions, the innocent packed in prisons,

Malcolm's phones tapped by snitches, false religion,

Pastors preachin' lies and pimpin' . . .

You already heard before what it was that I saw on the first two floors,

And on this third level I view, in my peripheral, the law, and boys in blue . . .

With they gats aimed . . . at me and you . . .

But . . . what exactly is it that we do?

Politicians yap about the freedom I have to speak,

But when I occupy the streets they send the riot police,

That's why we call 'em "the beasts," ain't no limit to what they can do to you,

That's why the first words the chief mouthed was "We shoot at you!"

I elevated, and this level was one I really hated . . .

A pastor passed a plate past the congregated masses' faces,

Waitin' for collections from poor people that paid it,

Separated humans by something man created,

He raked cake in, debated and stated I was heretical,

Raped kids, and then had the authority to bash homosexuals,

Straight bull dude, but he still can say, no play,

"I fool you!"

Why do I occupy?

Because when I look into my little sister's eyes, just before she cries, I see a
		pyramid lie

at the bottom of her iris . . .

And not the type made by my ancestors, Horus, Isis & Osiris; no . . .

From this, I get a different feeling; a sense of . . .

A broken educational system, embezzlement mission, materialism,

Greed and avarice, pure Capitalism . . .

Legislative reps make the law? Homie, you kiddin',

The government is run by lobbyists, who do the highest biddin',

Financial institutions and corporate entities run this country,

Enslave from cradle to grave for that money,

But the ultimate goal is bigger than that,

Colonization of your mind, then the map,

That's an actual fact,

Start wars and build prisons to do just that,

Got the media feedin' ya a bunch of bull crap,
You see they Capitalize off of capital lies,
So I capitalize my words to combat the Capitol's Eye . . .
And people afraid 2012 gon be when we die,
But if they ain't livin' every day like it's their last, why are they alive?
2012 is the beginning of the Age of Aquarius,
Only thing that's scary is,
The movement for change that is happening,
And only to those who enslave us,
The politicians, dictators, wicked rulers, banker,
Bloodsuckers of the poor get prepared,
'Cause we ain't gon be your slaves no more,
Since I got to the top floor at the top of the iris,
I've seen plenty of violence,
From unfair competition, self-centered individualism, loss of true vision, racism,
         lynchings,
Unfair court decisions, the innocent packed in prisons, Malcolm's phones tapped
         by snitches,
False religion, pastors preachin' lies and pimpin', a broken educational system,
Embezzlement missions, materialism, greed and avarice,
The essence of pure Capitalism . . .
And just as these men in suits prepare to say,
"We rule you!"
I cut 'em off and say, "I'ma let you finish,"
Well actually I'm not,
"But we gon have the greatest democracy of all time!
And if y'all keep trying
To stop us from occupying,
I say to Hell with these devils,
Let's set this joint on fire . . ."
Signed, the Occupier . . .

Occupation

By Olivia Weltz

17 years old

This is for everyone that walks the parameters of 15th and K Street
like they're looking at the primate house at the zoo.
Half laughing half pitying them for poppy-eyed idealism . . . asking
What good will erupt from the sod of the park grounds to be shot out of withering
        tents like landmines?
How can the banging rhythm pounding pumping beating
beat after beat in a circle of drums make them listen . . .
even for seconds?
And is it really possible to twinkle your fingers up to the sky to communicate with
        Kharma
demanding "No Justice, No peace, f the police"?
I really . . . can't say.
But I can ask you this.
What do you occupy?
And if you answered nothing, you should try it sometime.
Start by occupying your mouth by saying only what you think and telling only what
        you know.
Occupy your fists with sand when you raise them to fight to remind you how
        quickly rationality escapes us . . . all of us . . . whole countries of us.
Instead of concealed arms occupy your pockets with truth . . .
like the truth that guns kill.
Occupy your partner's hand with yours . . .
so they know you are there.
Occupy your lungs with sweet breath to remind them to keep pumping oxygen.
Because we're really all just made of molecules . . .
the same molecules
that constitute matter whose sole purpose it is to occupy air.
So if you're not occupying something what the hell are you doing?
Floating, orbiting, from point to point hitting each righteous asteroid that comes
        into your path . . .
but just floating on still.

If you don't occupy they will.

If you don't occupy how will anyone see your imprints like Neil Armstrong's on
       the moon?

And to the skeptics who look at the people on 15th and K and wonder why . . .
wonder why not.

Because these people live to occupy and take up space . . .use the life out of space . . .
and then breathe the life back into it by

beating the drums of peace because occupying is really the essence of our existence.

Feeling the gusts of change pass over your limbs . . .

through your pores . . . cleansing them of cynicism and doubt.

Because occupying is the way to tell the world

it may be dark but the light in you will brighten it

it may be big but so are you and you can change it

And anyone that cares enough for anything should be able to camp out for it . . .

drop out of the conventions that belittle them . . .

and occupy . . . be . . . exist.

Otherwise you're just a wasted occupation.

And the very foundations that make up the universe no longer apply.

The big bang made us because some particle erupted another,

being discontent with solitude . . .

so occupy to make yourself a part of something.

The more of us . . . the less of them.

The more we hold them accountable . . .

The more they count the syllables that come off their tongues.

If that isn't reason enough, then occupy yourself,

with people you love . . .

thoughts you love . . .

until you yourself are an occupation . . . breathing purity into your lungs . . .

a vessel . . .

An asteroid of change in the solar system.

I am the 99%

By Danny Crawford

26 years old

I am the 99%
Here I stand September 17 2011
Zuccotti Park in the Financial District
Trying to avoid another Depression
So yes I protest
Against social and economic inequality
High unemployment & greed
Damn they want every penny out of me
The gap between rich and poor
Is expanding at a fast pace
It's a special designed race
And we are in last place
The corporate influence on the government
Puts us at a disadvantage
They bail them out
Then kick our kids off of campus
Tuition increase
So we apply for a higher loan
For what?
Still can't get a job when we get home

I am the 99%
I march with my people
This is the land of the free
However no one is equal
Politicians with empty promises
It just fuels me with anger
Making side deals with each other
Leaving the middle class endangered
I get up and work hard every day
Making maybe $50,000 a year

Someone please tell me
Why I pay more taxes than a millionaire
Everything in America increases
With inflation it's hard to budget
How can you expect us to pay more
When our income doesn't

I am the 99%
My circumstances confirm it
The time to change is now
America deserves it

The 99% Is 100% Right
By Rocky Bright
25 years old

It was downtown, midnight, financial apocalypse
Salty police with pepper spray terrorized the occupants

Handcuffs and tough talk, curfew enforcement
Vacate the premises disassemble your voices

But not tonight commence to stand and fight
The 99% is 100% right

We work 60 hours weekly, but treated like Jonases
CEOs dismissed with massive cash bonuses

Jobs outsourced, our lives swing like a pendulum
Back and forth [their] bank accounts hidden in Switzerland

Tax breaks for the wealthy cut us in half
I pay more than billionaires now you do the math

As we stand united we will never fall
Until success is reached will be standing at City Hall

With a list of incentives to help and replenish
Our struggling workforce, the pursuit relentless

4.

Parents, Fatherhood

At 18 I Googled you.
—Nyles Thompson

Dave Zirin: How has your particular relationship as a parent shaped your writing?

Etan Thomas: It has completely changed my writing. I write about things that I would have never even thought to write about before, such as the birth of my first son Malcolm, coming home from a long road trip when my daughter Imani was just a few months old and her not remembering who I was, Malcolm crying for the first time when I told him I had to leave for a road trip, holding my youngest daughter Sierra for the first time in the hospital, the joys of seeing my children develop, take their first steps. I would say it just really expanded my writing

Dave Zirin: Is your poem that follows, "I Can't Wait to See You," based on true events?

Etan Thomas: Yes. I wrote this poem while my wife was pregnant with Malcolm. I just wrote all of the things that were going through my mind at the time. All of the questions, fears, the type of man I wanted him to be in the future, confessing that I will always be there for him—I just wrote it all.

Dave Zirin: A lot of the writing in this section deals with absent fathers. What concerns you most about the high number of children who grow up in single-family homes?

Etan Thomas: One of the things that concerns me the most is the message that a lot of adults are giving young people who are in that situation. They are spewing statistics at them and labeling them as being from a broken home, and crippled, and that they are probably not going to be successful in life. That is simply not true. Yes, it may be more desirable to have two parents in your home, but because you only have one doesn't mean that your life is over. You still can make the right choices and be successful in life. I just wish more adults were more positive with young people who are in this situation. I heard that same negativity when I was growing up in a single-parent household. There are just too many examples of great men and women who made the choice to overcome their situation and be successful.

I Can't Wait to See You
By Etan Thomas

I stare at your current home
A cramped quarters
You've stretched the borders
Making minds wonder if in there you are alone
Your movements make flesh expand in amazement
I picture you raising your clenched fist in protest
Stomping your feet to the voice of civil unrest
Maneuvering into different positions
You're restless
Vibrating to the pulsating sounds of your own beat
You've already got rhythm

I picture you smiling as you hear the advice
Pelted from every direction
Bombarding the ears of my wife
Attempts to accelerate your arrival
Castor oil and continuous squats
Soup that's hot
And walking around the block
Hot tea, climbing stairs and balancing steady
Little do they know that you'll come when you're good
And ready

Follicles above your crown burn your mother's heart
Birthing thoughts of tiny locks extending from your
Dome
Little ras

They say it's not possible
But in my mind roams the palatable perception of
Possibilities
NASCAR couldn't race faster than these thoughts that
Are dancing in my head
Sweeter than sugarplums
This journey has just begun

Malcolm
I can't wait to see you
An extension of me
Exhibiting distinct characteristics linking the bond
In our family
On your face whose features will I see?
Will you have your mother's lips?
My nose
Or her chin
I can't wait to gaze into the mirror of your soul
They say it's all in the eyes

The author of life has written your script many moons
Prior
And I'm forever grateful for my prize
The pride of a panther
My bundle of joy
A boy
A precious gift
As spirits are lifted through prayers and deep breaths
Pushing you into existence
Levels of elasticity never cease to amaze me
Expanding to the circumference of your horizon
Steadily rising to levels of supernatural

I rest on a mountain of clouded thoughts
Trying to avoid the storm harassing my serenity
An overcast of breached possibilities

Questioning the pounds that surround your flesh
Sending lightning rods of distress to lacerate my
Tranquility
I'm wet with too much knowledge
Meshed images of complications
Thundering through the forest of my mind
Resonating visions of torn sensations
I'm soaked with negative cases
How can I avoid the erasing of comfort in my soul?

The unknown and I were squaring off in a duel
Sworn enemies
He cradled fear as his secret weapon
Waiting for the right time to unleash his fury
He drew his sword drawing first blood

I turn toward the heavens
Asking my faith to extend to an infinite distance
Putting my trust in God
Confessing with my mouth
I'm speaking you into reality with persistence
The power of prayer

I pray God rains you into existence safe and sound

This must be heavenly sent
Holding on to a mentality that's spiritual
All natural forms of assistance
Blowing life through the living in itself is a miracle
The evidence of things not seen

I claim you as my me
The fruit of my loins
The glowing seed from the garden of me
That will blossom from the nutrients I instill in your
Mentality

You'll continue to grow regardless of the sun
Ignoring the melted morals that society's become
In the world but not of it
You'll conform to no one
Possessing the freedom to be yourself
Shielded from the arrows of adaptation
Unable to penetrate your skin
Reflected from the protection surrounding a secured
Mind
Connected to the resurrection possessed solely by the
Divine
And in Him you will pattern your life
Striving for a closer walk

You'll hear tales of the unfathered masses
Spreading like rashes across the ocean of normality
Rippling waves of fatherless seeds crashing to the
Shore of reality
As far as your eye can see you'll see
Dads that are gone with the wind
Creating lost sheep of fatherless children
Wandering aimlessly to an unfulfilled end
I'll never blow out of your life
With me you will have an everlasting bond
Singing songs of my daddy and me
I want you to look at me with pride
Riding waves of security
I wanna be the perfect illustration of how a father should be
An eternal connection interlaced to infinity
A continuous flame
A fire that will burn throughout the echoes of eternity

Lessons from My Mother

By Sieeda Jones

16 years old

Mama you always told me be a leader not a follower and if you going be a follower follow the right person. Did that apply to you, too? Because you sure ain't being a good leader right now. As I watched you get beat by your boyfriend over the years I thought to myself maybe that's why I got a low self-esteem, or maybe that's why I look at boys and love as something to fill that emptiness I feel in my heart. Mama, yes, you was always there for me but at the wrong times and I can't imagine the things you were doing and put before your daughter because you thought it was more important. It will take critical thinking and it will hurt my mind like you hurt my heart cus all the time I waited around for you to be a mother felt like time I was wasting, waiting around for my life to start. Mama, all the material things you gave me and all the babies, I'm sorry, will never make up for my insecurities and in the depths of my heart I have some type of hatred—well, dislike—for you cus I feel as though my life is all screwed up cus of the way you lived your life. I used to cry myself to sleep at night and write notes and put them on my pillow saying, Mommy, this spot is for you just to have that heartbroken feeling again to wake up in the morning and you was not there. That same heartbroken feeling I get when I put my trust into a boy, like I see you put all your trust into them low down dirty dogs that calls themselves men. It will be hard for me to be a good mother if I follow in the footsteps of you, and as you're chasing pavements I'm out here selling my heart to boys just to hear sweet words and feel a sweet kiss, and my soul turns into a shadow and disappears like you disappeared and tears was revealed, and I used my laughter and my smile as a shield, but my insides are screaming, Mommy, be here for me, love me, wipe the tears from my face, let me feel your warm embrace, cus if anyone was to kiss me the disownership rejection and abandonment they would taste. I'm just a baby girl in a teenager's body, in need of her mother's love. Sometimes I think, Did my father's death cause you to break down? Cus it sure broke me down. Then you lowered your standards and me watching you fall hurt and trying to pick you up brought me down. Maybe one day we'll meet up on the road of good mother and daughter relationship, cus now right now we're walkin' different paths and all I ever dream about is us being close again, closer than ever before, cus Mom, I love you, and I'm sorry for all the bad things I do, but just to let you know one reason I'm like this is because all the shit you put us through. I was a little girl trying to grow up too fast to take care of you, then reality caught up to me and Mom, I really need you. You'll always be the queen of my heart and in my eyes you're still the realest chick alive, and Mom, this is for both of us. At least for Sa'eed's sake we both need to live better lives.

A Drop of Rain from a Heart-Shaped Window Pain
By Chabre Woods
Age 23

"Ashley, Ashley, Mommy is screaming, help!" cried my little sister one night. To my surprise, I woke up to my parents engaging in a physical fight downstairs. I did not know what exactly was going on, but I tried my best to remain objective. I broke up a fight that ended in another sleepless night for my siblings and me. As predicted, my dad slept on the couch. On my way to school the next morning, my father told me the most horrifying news. Accompanied by affable tears, my dad informed me that they were getting a DIVORCE. I could see the hurt in his eyes but his tears were so friendly. I was already running late for school and then realized I had only five minutes to make it to the bus stop. As soon as I left, the rain quickly evolved from drizzles to showers. According to the local meteorologist, there was a zero percent chance of precipitation that day. My hair was wet, my clothes were soaked, and my umbrella was at home, leaving me with no protection from the raindrops.

The raindrops began to splash against my face, leaving a bitter aftertaste on my tongue. I finally made it to school, but I could not concentrate on anything. I could not tell my friends because they were too consumed in their lives and I knew they would not understand. They come from what I call happy families. Where did everything go wrong? What did I do to deserve this? What happened to our happy family? Discussing the divorce was something I could not do. Thus, I kept all my feelings bottled up inside. I felt powerless as if I had no control over this situation. My voice did not matter.

Later, my mother received custody of the kids. Taking sides is one of the most difficult side effects that children are forced to deal with. If you did not give Mom the same attention as Dad, there were consequences. I tried to help my sister adjust to the changes, but I could barely adjust to the changes.

After the divorce, my mom moved into an apartment. This apartment has so many silent memories that I have tried to erase over and over. Every time it rained, the raindrops were like knives cutting into my cheeks, only to cause my heart to start bleeding internally. At times, I felt like she hated us. She slandered my father fearlessly. Along with my heart, my ears began to bleed because the words were so hurtful. I remember many nights where I had to sneak and call my dad, making sure I erased my call log every time. Meanwhile, I spent a lot of time in my room simply watching the raindrops splash against my windowpane.

For years, I have dealt with feelings of guilt, anger, anxiety, depression, and jealousy. Unfortunately, my mother and I do not have the typical mother-daughter relationship. It is almost as if I am a chore to her sometimes. Her kids are like weapons in this never ending battle, while child support is her ammunition. The child support is not support for the child, instead it's a weapon used to create massive destruction in her children's hearts. While my father deals with this double taxation, his kids are scraping up items around the refrigerator to satisfy their hunger. From my understanding, child support is support for the child, not for the mother. Eventually, it came down to wanting to reside with the parent who could provide us with our everyday necessities as opposed to which parent was the coolest. I would say attention was the most expensive necessity that neither parent seemed to be able to afford at the time.

"Why don't you ask your dad, he has money?" "You should just go live with your dad. I'm done taking care of you. I did my part for 22 years." "Who do you like better, me or her? I'm your only mother."

These words found themselves drowning in my mind, gasping for air. Perhaps, if they had a life jacket maybe they could stay afloat and wouldn't hurt as much. I tried to conceal my feelings, but I was helpless. Anytime I come across a difficult challenge, these feelings seem to always resurface without warning.

Four years later, I found myself to be a Leadership Icon at my school. I was popular, smart, attractive, and the life of the party. Despite the fact that I was always smiling, I was slowly dying inside. I didn't understand—why did they look up to me? I was just being myself, exploring my passions and chasing my dreams. My self esteem level had dropped, causing me to not see what everyone else saw in me. Honestly, I wasn't happy with myself. How was I the president of an honor fraternity, but barely passing my classes? I was the life of the party, but was it because I was the most intoxicated? I will never forget the one summer I cried myself to sleep almost every night. I never knew someone who once had such high self esteem could feel so low. Where was everyone? Dad is too busy crunching numbers. Mom is too busy being bitter and spending everyone else's money. Grandpa is still adjusting to Grandma's death. My calls remain unanswered for days at a time as rent and tuition remain unpaid—one hotdog left and change in my bank account. At the time, all I wanted was to finish my degree even though I knew family attendance at my graduation would be low. My parents were so concerned with my grades prior to the divorce, and now I'm lucky if they know my major or how many A's I've received.

My senior year in college, I started suffering from anxiety attacks. I did not understand them or where they came from, but soon enough I found my own way of dealing with them. I avoided anything that I saw was causing stress on my life. Thus, I started removing class from my agenda and replacing it with happy hour. That was my method for preventing my attacks.

I started going to a counselor and she tried to get me to open up. My mouth was taped shut, and I only gave her enough information to get her to stop asking me questions. One day I finally opened up, but in an artistic manner. The rain started pounding against the windowpane in her office. Even worse, I still could not seem to find the perfect umbrella to keep me dry. She allowed me to notice how significant events from your past such as divorce can affect subsequent years of your life. Although there were some negative side effects from the divorce, I also embraced the positive side effects. Fortunately, I turned out to be highly independent, selfless, and discovered my potential, allowing me to become a great person and leader. Since my parents no longer motivated me to follow my dreams, I was blessed with the beautiful characteristic called self-motivation. Self motivation is precious because it allows you to channel the positive energy from within and only you reap the benefits as opposed to relying on external factors for happiness. Soon, all my happiness came from inspiring others regardless of my flaws and mistakes. I've received numerous awards and promotions, which I would not have received if my peers didn't think I deserved them.

More importantly, divorce has become a widespread issue across the nation. Preventing divorce may be a huge challenge, but helping children cope with divorce is essential, as they are the future of tomorrow. There are many kids that grow up without a father or mother in their households, and they are parched for love. Some teens turn to premature relationships when they are the most vulnerable, which can contribute to repeating the cycle of divorce. Survivors of divorce should give back and serve as a voice of reason. My aspirations include writing a book to help teens cope with divorce as well as starting a nonprofit organization in the latter stages of my career.

Growing up I had people like Malcolm X that I marveled at and held in high regard. Much more than simply putting a picture up or wearing a t-shirt, but actually looked up to and admired. It is an honor for me to present this next piece. This is a young man who has managed to turn his life around and whose namesake alone puts him in a special category. He is the grandson of Malcolm X. (Etan Thomas)

Untitled
By Malcolm Shabazz
22 years old

My mother (the 2nd eldest daughter of Malcolm X) is a so-called African-American, and my father is an Algerian-born Arab. They met each other in Paris, France, where I was born. My mother was there as a student, studying at the Sorbonne where my father was a professor . . . Without infringing too much upon their personal affairs, I'll say that differences arose early on between my parents, which led my mother to leave my father and return with me to the United States without even informing my father of her intention to do so.

Aside from my father's family, I am the grandson, namesake and "first male heir" of my grandfather (Malcolm X) from my mother's side. And my grandfather had six daughters, all of whom never married. So I was primarily raised within an extended family comprised totally of females.

Throughout my formidable childhood and early teenage years, the absence of my father or lack of any consistent male presence served as a source from which I wrongly harbored a lot of animosity towards my mother, our family, and others around me. I would find myself becoming envious and somewhat agitated at the sight of other children interacting with their fathers. And I would often cut up and act out due to an unawareness of how to otherwise express my feelings of abandonment and neglect. Growing up I actually did snap, and many times my misbehavior was intentional. When I look back, I feel that a lot of the mistakes that I made in life could have been avoided if only I had that consistent positive male figure to help steer me in the right direction.

I've learned to never regret or curse any particular situation or circumstance though. For it is these obstacles which only serve to make us stronger, just as coal under extreme pressure makes the transformation into diamond, or "no pain, then no gain," as others would say. Experience is the best of teachers. And while knowledge is simply to know-the-ledge through familiarity or awareness, wisdom is that acquired knowledge tested—through trial, error, and tribulation—to bring about the best of understanding. What is evident is that most people are like tea bags—not worth much until they've been through some hot water.

My grandfather—Malcolm X—once stated that there are only two types of power that are respected within the United States of America—economic power and political power—and that social power derives from those two . . . The great revolutionary George Jackson stated that "so-called criminals and crime arise from economic, material and socio-political causes."

So if it's at all true that we are somewhat products of our environments, then I suppose it would explain our current predicaments, the events which led up to these points and why we had ever been as we were or currently are in thought and through action. However, it's neither necessary nor beneficial that we run down lists of ills that may have affected us in one way or another. We may be placed in many undesirable situations, yet we alone make the decisions, which produce the consequent outcomes.

We often find ourselves in positions where we wish that we could turn back the hands of time, where we wish to go back and do things differently. Time-travel isn't a reality. So the only remedy is to be as conscious as possible in the present. The past isn't to be dwelt upon, but rather to be looked to as a road map or compass in the present that can help us successfully navigate into the future.

Like my grandfather—Detroit Red—I wasn't raised in the streets, but was akin to a moth attracted to the bright lights. I went through my own rebellious phase between the age of nine through 22, and I am now 25 years old. There are over 13 dead Homies that I still think about to this day, countless Comrades who will never again see the light of day, and even mothers who will no longer speak to me because they believe their sons to be deceased or incarcerated in my name. Given all of this, I couldn't even begin to describe what it takes for me to keep tickin' knowing that my own grandmother passed away due to my reckless actions at the age of 12 years.

I only share to express that I too have been around the block. There comes a time in our lives when we must change our views and improve upon our ways. As we get older we must mature. Otherwise we become stagnant. As people of color, we have moral obligations to upgrade our lifestyles. We're not gangsters, thugs, or any of that. We all make mistakes. Some of us more than most. However, those of us who made more mistakes should be in a position where we have learned the most. For it is insane to repeat the same mistakes expecting different results.

A famous Muslim scholar once said that if his prosecutors imprisoned him, then his cell would become a place of worship . . . I only say this to express that my own time spent in prison (five years) wasn't served in vain. I did the time, rather than allowing it to do me. The universal element of time is mastered according to how one utilizes it. In order to master this element, one must at the very least strive towards mastering the "Self." So during my own bid I made a conscious effort to not just merely change my ways and actions, but rather to strive towards broadening, reshaping and expounding upon my entire perspective and thought process.

A great Vietnamese general by the name of Ho Chi Minh once declared: "When the prison gates are opened, the real dragon will fly out!"

Running Without Legs
By Judith Angeles
26 years old

run without legs, I try
to leave myself wrapped in
shouts and screams, don't want
to argue my way out,
so I run without legs
to a destination of swaying
wet trees, pushed by a
thunderstorm too loud to care
that I'm drenched and tired,
paled from hard paced breaths
of running without legs,
longing to be a ghost—
invisible from the pain I
can't stay dry from. beaten
won't bruise, since I'm a
rock drowning in the currents of
my eyes.
Yet I smile throughout the lashes
like a phoenix, I know I'll rise
from my ashes—when love
scorches my chest up
burning alive a plaque
older than me,
a disease, epidemic in
my families' names,

mixed up by too many
last names, not of my father.
for running without legs
leaves me defenseless to
the night.

Papa Stayed at Home
By P Philosophy
19 years old

You remember sitting on the couch
waiting on the news
—Anxious
When you heard those words
—I'm pregnant
you didn't know to be happy or . . .
The only thing you knew was solid
was your life from this point on would change

You watched the pregnancy
Amazed at the fact that your seed grew into a baby
in someone else

The day came
You paced and waited
supported and pushed aside your own fear
and prayed to God for everything to end well

When you finally held your baby
Any fear you had was replaced with wonder
for the years to come and a fierce protectiveness

You defied statistics
and took your place in an overlooked group

appreciating people's acknowledgment
of your love for your child
but letting it roll off
because to you it's being there for the milestones
that rewards you
the unexpected hug and I Love You Daddy
that lets you know responsibility
can   feel   so   good

I want to let you know
I See You

You make parenthood look so good
your boys say they can't wait
to be blessed with their own joy
watching the way your little one's eyes
light up at the sight of you

I never knew a diaper bag
could make a man look sexier
But my whole point is
I See You

I know it must be frustrating
to be collected into a group
and put down by movies and TV
and these statistics
you've never seen one person
in the hood observing and collecting

You've dealt with trips to Friend of the Court
and never got treated friendly
fighting to know the truth
because this bundle of joy has stolen your heart
and nothing can hurt more than being told
you don't have a right to love him any longer

I know you struggle to keep your nine to five
taking disrespect you wouldn't in the street
to achieve a little paper

I understand the struggle
just because one month
you had only love to give
doesn't make you a deadbeat
Don't worry
your child knows you're there and you care

You've put all your hope into their upbringing
given up dreams so they can have theirs
I want to say Thank You
but it seems so little
because I know
you're just doing you
But again

I just wanted to say
I See You

They Don't Listen
By Joe Rosga
12 years old

Sometimes it just sucks to be a kid. Your parents don't listen to you when you want
them to, and listen when you don't want them to. My parents are divorced and I do
not get to see my dad as much as I would like to. One day I asked my mom if we
could reverse the schedule that we had already set, that way I would be living with
my dad. What my mom told me was that this is not your decision, it is for me and
your father to decide. I said well, shouldn't the child get a say in it?

Shouldn't the one who is actually living the situation have some type of say? She
said yes but that is not the way things work. She also told me that although I did

61

bring up a good idea, she doesn't need to agree with me on it. I felt like the conversation was more of a debate than a mother to son type of talk. I didn't give up though, I kept fighting and fighting to get what I wanted, but she wouldn't break. She had a comeback for almost everything I said. It was like she knew it was coming. After our hour long conversation (debate) I was so mad that I went straight to bed. No dinner, didn't brush my teeth, didn't care about watching TV, just went straight to bed. That's why sometimes it just sucks to be a kid. Parents won't agree with you or listen to you.

Little Rock
By Rocky Bright
25 years old

It was nine months, anticipation of a new life
Settle into a new home with my old friend, my new wife
Prenatal conversations underneath the moonlight
Create the perfect reincarnation of D Bright

A lullaby every evening to stimulate your mental
MP3 heavenly played soft instrumentals
As I reminisce with my pen, you should have seen my eyes when
I knew you were strong because you kicked like Ninja Gaiden

I was at the doctor's office and began this soliloquy
Possibly a few issues, a complicated delivery
I wasn't worried because your birth would complete the trilogy
I trust in medicine but my faith endures biblically

Prepare for and expect the best, for what it's worth
Your bedroom was finished three months before your birth
Received love from our families, never did the drought hit
Gifts in abundance, your closet full of outfits

I thought about my friends who weren't ready or willing
Never witnessed the development of their children
They say it's not an issue, I know that's a lie

A hole in their souls big enough to drive a semi

November 4th 2:27 in the afternoon
A child so precious came forth from the womb
Your lungs filled with oxygen and cleared out the room
Singing a song unknown, but I enjoyed the tune

Your mother displayed courage, we will never drift apart
Sacrifice and valor, she deserves a purple heart
Nurses took care of you, gave you a naked rinse
I knew you were special because they brought myrrh and frankincense

You are a piece of my heart, not yet tattered or bruised
I will give my full support whatever route you choose
As long as I breathe, no one will dishonor thee
You can enjoy athletics or excel in astronomy

Fresh out of the gate six pounds ounces eight
Facial features a perfect blend of two soul mates
The economy is down but I found joy in the aftermath
I went to work this morning clutching your photograph

In a life of monotony it was hard to maintain
But when my dreams began to smolder you rekindled the flame
Unaware of your strength, welcome home son
Beneath the Sun a new chapter has begun.

Little Man
By Sarah Hillware
17 years old

Right now, I'm looking at a lantern . . . with a small burning fire
That has the desire . . . that the world desires to have,
I'm sitting here just staring at the flame, so I've decided to give it a name, "little man."
That little man is burning, just burning away,

63

But fire turns into smoke, so little man knows he will not be able to stay . . .
in his burning fire form,
Any minute now, the rain from the storm can blow him away.

The rain that comes from divorce, abuse, domestic violence, adultery . . .
The hell on earth that, already, little man has had to bear,
He had no choice, for he was born into a life that is not fit for anyone . . .
Because his mother was an escort,
His father only comes around to see him when it's his last resort,
And all little man knows is how men throw women against the wall as a sport,
Little man hardly learned his ABCs and 1,2,3s
But he learned how to reel the broads in and use his body parts to appease,
And he doesn't know the names of the itchy red bumps, but he knows he has a
          disease,
And it makes the little man wonder . . .
"So why am I living anyway?"
He burns to live and lives to burn.
I'll truly never understand this flame.
This flame is a little boy who grew up to be a man who wishes his mother would have
JUST aborted him anyway,
Little man is no longer little on the outside, but the flame in his soul grew small
          and he no longer
Stands tall,
His head is low and now he's all alone in this oppressive world with nowhere to go,
Except for her arms, in between her legs, to create ANOTHER flame
That will eventually get smaller . . . and smaller . . . and smaller, and eventually die
          out.
Because in order to keep a fire burning, you must have wood . . .
Because in order to bring a child up right in this world, you must have love: the
          unconditional kind.
And love needs two halves to burn, because Supermother can't do it alone.
Because little man needs both halves, he burns . . .
He burns for a mother who cares enough to tell him that he has a place in her life,
A father who is there, teachers who tell him that he can,
Social workers who tell him that there is hope.

And so long to the love that used to be,
So long to the staples of society,
Because little man does not see any deviation in sight from wasting his life,
To him, there IS no option or variety.

So why is your flame still burning anyway?

Promises
By Ayana Jenkins
18 years old

Broken promises
Unrecognized signs
Different perceptions
Alternate recollections
What was this ever about?
Many let-downs
Patterns were formed
You become used to it
It's something like the norm
You put on a smile
But in your mind you wonder how
Oh what's just one more broken promise?
I tell you about my play
You say hey what's the day?
I tell you with glee
But then I remember how you can be
I promise myself not to get let down
But I'm instantly filled with mirth at the prospect of a turnaround
So on the night of the play I make a promise to do my very best
But I'm assured I can't keep it when my mother doesn't show up
No change
No progress
Oh what's just one more broken promise?

F*** a Dad I Never Had

By Nyles Thompson

19 years old

Since day one it was my mom and me
Mom is skinny, choosing to feed me—checks only go so far
Living in the room of another person's house
It's too cold—my lungs begin to close—
Near death, saved by an injection at the hospital my mom cannot afford

Toddler me sitting on the couch, phone to ear—
a strange man's voice is on the other end
Confused, I set it down and run off to play—
After all, what do I know of him?

This man who apparently is my dad keeps sending cards—
full of false hope and promises—
Wish he'd send some food,
so my mom could eat until she was full . . .
We get a box of cheese and some cheap hair clips—
the government does more than this.

Paycheck to paycheck, thank God for the credit card
Rolling pennies on the way to the gas station
"Pray we make it," she'd often say . . . and I did
I used to sit in that Ford Escort and pray so hard I'd nearly give myself a headache

New school year, new clothes—on credit
Pick some you can make last—
no way was I getting what all the others had in the class
Thrift shop, consignment shop, but don't let them know—
"Have PRIDE," she would say . . . I hate that damn word to this day
Always felt I didn't have to prove anything to anyone but self—
But to be different is to be ridiculed, so I often shut my mouth

Rich school, rich kids . . . but I was not one
Waking up at 5 am, time to go to the babysitter—
She was the bus driver
Waking for a second time in a stranger's home
Always the first to board the bus—I knew the whole route

Always the extra one in the bunch—
babysitter to babysitter, how I resented those families
.Constantly told what to do by people who were not my mother—
Accused of things I never did and used as a maid service every Saturday

In middle school curiosity came—
wondering about this man from a foreign land
Who am I?
Where do I come from?
Where did my legacy begin?
Resentment towards my mom—I've decided she kept me from you,
She is the reason for the disconnect in my cultural identity . . .
But still contemplating how someone could let me go so easily.

Tears across the years
My grandmother cried from Istanbul while I cried in Seattle—
I couldn't understand how someone could not want me—
their flesh and blood
Married into America—false pretense for citizenship—
Wish they had denied you,
before you could have had the chance to break my mother's heart . . .
Maybe then you'd understand how it feels to be kept outside.

At 18 I Googled you
Found you lived in the States
Four years—four trips only because of your girlfriends' attempts
to make me part of the family
Out of sight—I always seem to be out of mind
Only hear from you occasionally—
hate how you ignore me,

but figured no point in speaking on something you won't acknowledge

I've always held my tongue—
tried to forgive what cannot be changed—
accept people for where and who they are—
Unrealistic expectations only result in more disappointment

Excuses and fantasies are all you ever offered me
years of promises to meet the family—
funny how your ex and her daughter met them before me—
Finally I was able to manage without you, connect with my family—
Was unable to speak without translation, but some things do not need words—
we spoke with smiles and long embraces

You are the dad I never had, but you damn for sure aren't my father
I have been infected with the self-hate and animosity
most children unwanted by their fathers take a lifetime to disassemble
Time can ease it, but it refuses to erase it
Forever etched in my heart is an imprint of rejection—
your refusal to project emotion—
to reach beyond the barriers I never created
to reconcile with the one you brought so carelessly into this world—
but I refuse to be taken out in the same manner . . .
I will not be bonded by chains of sadness because you fail to bond with me.

A Father's Prayer
By Danny Crawford
26 years old

Watch them my Lord
For you're the one that sees all
Protect them from evil
Pick them up if they fall
Circumstances restricted me as a father
From being a physical presence

So I am here on my knees
Asking my Father to step in
I was feeling helpless
Powerless, almost defeated
Until I realized faith in God
Was all I needed
I went from seeing my children
On a consistent basis
Then suddenly to having to get a court order
Just to see their faces
Now I have to be to court on time
Just for them to tell me to wait
Then the mother doesn't show up
So they set another date
Thirty days from today
Thirty more days without seeing my children
So pardon my tears as they drop
When I walk out of that family court building
Pardon my frustration, my anger
At the fact she didn't show up for court
But she was the first one in line
For that child support
And these are my feelings
Imagine what the kids are going through
Wondering where's Daddy?
Them boys are suffering too
All I can do is pray
And never use the word can't
'Cause God will deliver
So I thank him in advance

A CANCERous Growth: Ashes to Ashes

By Pages d. Matam

24 years old

On my first day of middle school in English class
My teacher asked for proper introductions by having everyone tell
Their name and what they'd want to grow up to be
I really wanted to answer something cool like all the other kids
A banker, athlete, or even sanitation engineer
But what I really wanted to say was that
Ever since I was 8 years old I've wanted to grow up to become a cigarette
Because it was the only thing that my father could never abandon
I've never smoked a cigarette because I was afraid
Of finding a father figure in a pack of Marlboros
For as long as I can remember, I've felt like a man constantly in reverse
Like the backwash of a dream, like Karma's favorite crash test dummy
Constantly begging someone for all the love they have already given me
Started drinking and being with women to fill the potholes in my spirit
But drinking more Absolut only made me more obsolete
Now I'm just a soul made with 50% recycled plastic
That hugs so tight because it makes pretending that letting go is never an option
　　　　easier
An assembly of a man who loves like a runaway locomotive.
My tears still tending to the Lazarus pieces of broken women buried in my collarbone
As I treated their orgasms like mirrors for me to convince myself I was beautiful

When I was 13, I first started building train tracks on my stomach, some on thighs
To all the parts of me I wished I could forget
But this only made me more of a swollen dirty pile of remorse
A shotgun shell in a waiting room of catastrophe
With a fiendish appetite for earthquakes at the dripping enjambment of a woman
The earth shifts between my teeth and does not return the same
Misshapen planets have always tasted better to me
There is no gravity to my will
Only cadence and a vulgar smile stitched to a sense of humor

Hiding the boy with the skin of a scarecrow
Because it's the only way his corny heart can ward off the birds and the bees

The only thing my father ever passed to me
Is this uncanny ability to hurt the people we love the most
In a split second, I lost the only woman that I ever truly loved
The very next year on a random doctor's visit I found out that I was alcohol intolerant
I've drunk so much over the years that liquor has became poisonous to my blood
And my next shot could very well be my last
You know God has a funny sense of humor
Took away the two things I harbored on the most
To teach me that liquor and women are not a cure to my loneliness

So what do you want to be when you grow up?
I answered . . . I want to be a pediatrician, one that helps save and heal children
Starting with myself
But who would've known that more than a decade later
I'd make a stethoscope out of a microphone
Write poems like daily prescriptions and turn the stage
Into a patient room for the healing to start within
Because searching for the divine in yourself often leads to
The harsh realization that you've been more rick james than first james
With built in fire escapes inside your bones
For the times you want to run away from yourself

I used to want to grow up to become a cigarette
Made sense because I'm a cancer
But no chemotherapy to my astronomy
I radiate as a magnanimous collage of comic books, plantains and electric sound
As a sun afraid to shine, but always willing to give all of his light
To save anyone's sunset, which is all but the excruciating reality
That I don't want to die alone and only be remembered as a small escape
With a slow burning pulse, kinda like a cigarette.

5.
Relationships

I packed my bags today.
All I left him was a tear-stained pillow, soaked in the
painful confusion released from the eyes whose glow
once belonged to him.
—Chaina N. Dobbins

Dave Zirin: The poem by your brother Julian, "Don't Talk to Me About Love," suggests that love is best realized through struggles. Do you agree with him?

Etan Thomas: I'm not an expert but I know that love is filled with ups and downs. I know that, as Julian said in his poem, it's not all "wine and roses." I think the point of his poem is that true love conquers all—that love doesn't disappear at the first sign of struggle, but that it withstands the pitfalls of life and is victorious.

Dave Zirin: In your experience speaking with teens what has surprised you most about their perception of love?

Etan Thomas: What surprises me is that some teens have such deep and complex relationships where they feel that they are so deep in love at such an early age, but really they have no idea what love really is. Some I have spoken to have that deep feeling about one person the first semester, then have that same feeling about someone else the next. But on the other hand, I have also been surprised at how many struggles and dramatic experiences some young people have had at such an early age, which you will see in some of the writings that follow.

Dave Zirin: Do you think parents are aware of some of these "struggles and dramatic experiences" their kids are going through?

Etan Thomas: Unfortunately, I don't. From what I have seen, a lot of parents have no idea what their kids are going through, and a lot of kids don't share with their parents. Some of their issues and problems are far beyond anything that most adults can even fathom that their little 16-year-old son or daughter is dealing with. Writing about it is a good way to express those feelings.

Don't Talk to Me About Love
By Julian Thomas
30 years old

don't talk to me about love in the beginning

you wait until things get rough

when the passion is gone
and the dream is deferred

only then can you talk to me
about love

one to one
like a true man

don't talk to me about love when it's all wine and roses

chocolates and sweet nothings to get me through the night.

when it's all stolen glances and foot massages
candlelit dinners and Sandra Bullock movies
massage oils and incense and Coltrane and headboards

and don't get me wrong, i dig that stuff too
but that ain't the time to talk about love

you wait just a little while longer
wait until things get rough

talk to me about love when i'm out of luck
and you're out of work
and the rent's due
and the bills are late

talk to me about love when you're too proud to stand in line for a check
or i'm late for a job interview and the bus don't show

talk to me about love when the lights are cut off
when we've pawned your gold watch and my silver trumpet
when the neighbors are talking and the church members gossiping
and at candlelit dinners we toast bologna sandwiches

with no mustard

then you can talk to me about love
talk to me about love when our plans have died
when you're too busy to start up that business
and i'm too tired to go back to college

when the heat's cut off again and there's a leak in the roof,
and the health insurance won't cover a damn thing

talk to me about love when your parents hate me

when your pastor won't counsel us
because i'm southern baptist
and you're devout methodist

when my uncle is drunk at our family reunion
and the kids act a fool and the in-laws keep arguing
and the bbq's burnt cause I never did like your mama's cookin no way,

that would be a good time to start talking to me about love

don't talk to me about love in the beginning

cause baby, that's just too easy
you wait just a little bit longer
to talk to me about love

when you can't stand my voice
and i can't stand your smell
when your teeth have gone yellow
and my love handles sag

talk to me about love when the car payment's due
and the price of diapers has gone up again.
when the overcrowded school is just not good enough
for our attention deficit daughter
or our son that's considering gang protection

talk to me about love when we're out marching for freedom
and our cell phone taps are clicking in the background

when our weekly trips to the open mic spot just don't cut it no more

talk to me about love when they come for me in the night

when one of us is on the run
and being hunted down for covert tactics
against a suppressive central power
that used to be a democracy
and now is just demon crazy

the kind of love that whispers through steel bars
and cries through plexiglass
cause your voice just don't sound right
on these tattered prison phones

the kind of love that waited for Mandela
that waited for Malcolm
and that waits for Mumia even now as we speak

don't talk to me about love in the beginning
that's the easy part

you wait until things
get good and rough.

and then,
and only then
can you talk to me
about love

Weathering
By Aja Monet
22 years old

I.

When the earth shatters
beneath us
  and we are
broken   open
picked
    apart
by the silence
Let me tell you:
You are unrehearsed laughter
sleeping between the murmur of my lips
an unconscious love,
a man dipped in midnight lightning
I will fix my body for you
and fold
  in the bend
of your arms,
a tortured jewel.

You are a freedom song humming
in the shadow
of my soul,
a healing heartache
    that kisses wounds
and sets free tornadoes
on my spine such a c r i p p l i n g tongue.
for the small pleasure
  of your mouth,
a delicious
thunder
on my collarbone
I am grateful
to
    whatever heaven
awaits us
My spirit is
  dancing
in the gospel
of your chest
and I
have found music
    glowing
in the whirlwind
of your eyes
may we create new skies
to fall apart under,
together.

II.

You are a steady storm
a street light trembling
a field of shivering buildings
a rusted goodbye pressed gently against the ear.

Whisper me a hurricane,
you are the flood.
You are the knuckles of trees
set aflame.
You are the sky's shoulder blades breaking
a cloud threading open,
the aftermath
a chandelier of fire tilting in my eyes
every time you leave.

Saved by Knight
By P Philosophy
19 years old

A knight in shining armor
fortified with words
He comes to still the night
and brings with Him
a light encased in His banner

No more midnight cries and black eyes
Fighting
for an impossible goal

Because in the end
the Dark Knight the damsel fights
has only been responding to the voices
of His own nightmare

She was never privy to His reason
so She lived in the Dark

Her only comfort was to learn to fight
He was a good teacher
if not a companion

Pain and night came to share the same definition
Prayers were written and burned
She feared even voicing them silently
would imprint it on Her soul
and raise the Darkness's question
of "Do You Love Me?"
Prolonging Her life with more lies
She always utters "yes"
while staring into a glitter of a knife

Now this White Knight comes
with pretty words
to uplift the spirit

Or is it a clever attempt to break
down the wall built
to protect what was left of self
and keep it hidden while
She existed in the dark

Why break down heavy built defenses
You come with pretty words
White Knight
like any poet

But so did He

What makes you different
from that Night
to make you My Knight

You may wear a different color
but anything can be disguised
Why should I not
exist in familiarity
at least I can recognize these blows

NO,
DON'T GO!

Even with fear and hurt
leaving me questioning you
don't leave My Knight

I will die here
encased in this tomb
if you leave me
to reside in the deafening dark
of this Knight.

I'm Good at Holding In My Emotions
By Maurice Clark
19 years old

So I'm good at holding in my emotions . . . I'm good at holding back the fact that the first girl I ever loved don't love me anymore . . . Doesn't want to feel my touch anymore, doesn't want to kiss and fall into a world of bliss, NO she doesn't miss that anymore . . . With how many times she has been hurt I would never guess that the muscle under her breasts would leave me for dead. I remember we said we would never hurt each other and we both lied, but why does it feel like she lied more? Why does it hurt to the point of physical pain that she is pushing me out of her veins? You see I used to be her bloodstream. I used to run thru her heart mind and soul every second of the day and she would smile and whisper she loved me when we would play teenage games like "find the closest place to park dot, dot, dot" you can fill in the blanks . . . But now we don't even speak we don't text we don't FB we don't even email. And she will never admit to hurting me but she knows that without her I'm nothing more than lonely and a lot less than something. And I keep a smile on my face trying to hide ANY TRACE of hurt or pain! "What up Mingo?" "What it do Man?" I guess I'm good at holding in my emotions. But the constant roller coasters that my mind goes thru are making me feel like I'm on ice in the middle of the ocean in ninety degree weather . . . I can't even swim. Whoever said true love is timeless was high. And that doesn't rhyme but I can't believe that lie cuz our love was true! Our love grew, our love was the equivalent of a fairy tale come true, and now it's gone and I let water run down my face. Alone as I write poems but no one will ever know how I feel because I guess I'm good at holding in my emotions.

The Huntress
By Chaina N. Dobbins
21 years old

I packed my bags today.

All I left him was a tear-stained pillow, soaked in the painful confusion released from the eyes whose glow once belonged to him.

These eyes used to be my glory: a huntress's greatest weapon when hunting for the most prime and challenging game. When they caught his they trapped him like a netted lion tricked into bondage while searching for water in the south Saharan desert he calls home.

Bright whites barely seen beneath wide irises enticed and flagged him down. Irises so deep and tempting he nearly drowned in the brown. Pupils so sharp they cut him loose from his natural trappings while originating one anew. And lids whose closings were the scariest thing he knew because he quickly became accustomed to these eyes.

Look again.

I had done my research: lions have such sharp claws, thick fangs and hungry will-power that taming them is a fantasy and simply holding them is a temporary illusion in itself. And he was the most typical of lions: confidently regal and not easily maintained. Yet somehow the way he slyly sauntered into what I thought was my possession persuaded me that I had done the impossible. The way he knowingly partook of the nutrients I provided him, daily mouthing them from the palms of my hands, convinced me that he would never seek to feed himself again. And his purr. Alone it comforted my belief that I had finally found my final prize. I could now retire; my days as a huntress were over. But when paired with the ferocity of his roaring aggression it confused me into thinking there was even more to him than meets These eyes.

I now see these eyes were in fact my curse: what I thought was a secret weapon for containing wild royalty was in fact a signal that tagged me as an easy target. He grasped my glance in his and like opposing magnet ends we melded by no force of our own. But we were so alike: both fearless, both hungry, both unashamedly vicious in our rectifications of disorder in our kingdoms. We were too alike. In fact, we were nearly identical. No wonder we ended up repulsing in the end.

Unlikely companions turned into the best of friends. And then remiss. Eyes once glossy with glow too quickly turned arid with emptiness.

I found him in the desert. Thirsty. Searching for water. I suppose he found what he was looking for; these eyes held more water than I could ever have imagined possible. But now I give him his last and dearest desire, pouring out my waters upon his bedsheets until I have nothing left. But what I came with:

These eyes.

Heart Breaker
By Desiree Coker
16 years old

There is no shame
When he plays his game
He feels no pain
Because there is no shame
His eyes will wander
His lies will grow
And every time he talks to you
He is letting her know
He says to her
"Oh she's nothing"
In return he tells you
"Girl you're stunning"
You hear these things
And you see his ways
But yet you stay
Everyone sees your pain
But you say they're insane
He calls you names
You say he doesn't mean
But your heart is steadily ripping
Then one day he calls

He says he has it all
With you he won't lose
And you know that he is lying
But you go along sighing
Then three days later
You catch him cheating
You feel your heart stop beating
And the sadness that hits
Makes you want to quit
He calls to stay
"I love you baby"
Then you tell him it's over
Making you want to be sober
You lie down that night in tears
Wishing the end was near
But then you realize
He was nothing in your eyes
He was the love faker
The beautiful heart breaker

Take Me Away: It's hard to love
By Daryl Fortson
20 years old

It's hard to love a man so closely linked with insecurity, and out of touch with reality, with the reality of his children, with the reality that he's really lost one. Refuses to really listen when she says she's heard it all before, that she's been hurt, and refuses the repetition of this process that you relay so relentlessly.

It's difficult to be truthful with a man who doesn't know it himself. Who refuses to realize that truth is universal, not by individual standards. Truly, I tell him, his plots for peace only serve as ammunition in this war, and his paranoia and self-absorption is only fuel for friendly fire.

We are no longer friends. I'm tearing down all fronts, putting myself and my loved ones first. Although I realize that you, to an extent, are still one of them, I'm sorry; you're further down the list, for your actions have failed and will fail to win you back the daughter you think you know, and will only succeed to distance yourself from the only biological child you have left, leaving you to make some decisions: Will you broaden your mind and expose yourself to a truth that islarger than your own? Can you learn to trust in the notion that maybe it's really not about you? That maybe it could have been if not for the rose-colored glasses that is your alternate reality? Maybe, if you tried, you would be easier to love.

The Tap
By Alexander Miller
23 years old

What shall we do,
When it whispers to us,
The faintest sound, a syllable,
In your ear?
It taps at your shoulder,
Inconsiderate of time,
Whether it is, or not, yours

A convention of souls,
Two, to be exact,
Brought together,
By chance? Fate?
Or did one seek out the other
By some attraction, based
On love of intellect, wit, a perfect
Charming
Line in the face?
What brings you to another?
The burly definition of deltoids,
The slender, delicate hips, the line of the spine,
And the texture of her skin,
Get most of us to muster the
Courage to summon another to the altar
For the eternal bond

But some
Are not so easily moved,
And have a harder time
Answering the tap, the
Whisper,
Requiring many windy
Nights and stars in the
Nebulae, for the spell
To be cast upon them

What of them?
What shall we do
When we are called
To meet another?

Three Poems
By Eric Taylor
20 years old

Love Is...

Living for others' happiness. It cannot be bought. It is not a prize to be won. Love is tangible. Love is Mother's. It is found in children. It can change the world. God is love. He told us to give it to one another. It must be given regardless of your religion. Love is service. Love is charity. It's moving past others' mistakes. Love is optimistic. Love is why we are awake. Love is not just a word—it's a symbol. Love is contagious. Love is power. Love is life.

We Are One

We are one. You and me. Me and you. We ride together. Side by side in this fight for life. Never shirk the work. Obedience till immortality. Without a doubt we will succeed. I got your back. We will not stop. We will fly high. We will not stoop low.

Step by step side by side. All we know is go. Out mouths will not be silenced. The Ghost will not be hidden. The light will shine through the darkest night. He is love. We are brother. We are sister. We are zealotry. We are one.

Switch

I'm groping through the mist. Searching out the fallen. Blind to the word but listen to the heart. Awkward for awkward I aim to proclaim. Take the hand, change the game, break the chain. Ignite the flame. Blast off to light. No longer of this world. Not the trap. Not the girl. New train of thought. Full steam ahead with this caboose I wrought. His word is his bond, live for his work and sing his song. Tried to dance with the devil, now you salsa on another level. When I am bound and beat with poison I'm forced to eat I learn the greatest lesson in jail at liberty.

The Intervention
By Tamara Sease
26 years old

I was dating a boy in high school who broke up with me after I told him that I was not ready to have sex. This poem is a conversation God had with him on my behalf.

Good morning, My son.
I am fully aware of all the plans you have today, primarily because I am not in-
        cluded in them.
But I must interrupt you for a time as this.
I have an urgency that must be fulfilled through dialogue with you about My daughter.
Please note that the only portion of this dialogue I require of you to share is "Yes."
So listen.
You are loved.
Few words will ever express that adoration I have for you.
When I shaped and molded and structured your being, I knew the end result as
        you began life in your mother's nest.
Yet, just as much as I love you, there is someone else who holds My affection as well.
She was also formed in My likeness.

From her smile to her laugh, I knew, just as you, the finality of her disposition, the
destination of her journey, the reward at the end of her pursuit.
But, just like those times of tenderness and bliss, every tear she cries that falls
from her eyes would embody Me.
You cannot fathom the extensity of anguish I feel when she does.
Therefore, I have made a point to fight for her.
I am not here to unleash wrath or anger upon you; we both know the ending of that.
I am just here to adjust your focus and provide clarity on the woman you cannot see.

She is a boatload of insecurities sailing through a sea of doubt.
Her mind is often a tumbleweed, bouncing through dry deserts I've allowed as the
key elements of her life she will need to survive as she progresses toward
maturity.
She loves harder than she receives and when loneliness haughtily arrives at her
door, she struggles to understand its presence and plummets through an
abyss of despair.
But today I am moving My heaven and earth for her.

Trust, I am not surprised how the frigidness of your heart unexpectedly shunned
her out as you force-fed her illustrations of a hope she longs for.
Nor am I astounded or amazed at the typical ultimatum you've placed at her feet; I
knew that you would.
She didn't.
But My Son has whispered her and wrapped her up in a compassion of content-
ment you will never understand.

Nothing Will Keep Us Apart
By Charles Kent
19 years old

I don't need any smoking mirror to bring you nearer from across the country
I can close my eyes and imagine you into existence
Even if I can't physically touch you
I can feel your connection to my soul
But that's nothing

I can retreat to my thoughts and chase your suffering away
Even if the cause is looking me in my mirror
And it's clearer than ever that far too often I've been the cause of your happiness
        turning to tossing and turning throughout the night
Sleepless
Wrestling with thoughts to frighten you
And even if you halfway bought my explanations
Your mind can't keep from turning to worst-case scenarios
I'm sorry I've ruined how you view me
I know in the past I've let you down
But as long as I'm around
You will always have my heart
I've started to change a new leaf
I've parted the crease in the jeans of my personality
And I will be less selfish
You are that important to me
I don't care what your parents say
I know I make you happy
We've all made mistakes
So he who is without sin . . .
But not to escape my original point
I long for you to return to me
Like slumdog millionaire I am holding onto hope like "Yes We Can"
You will always have my heart
They can't destroy our bond
Like Romeo and Juliet
We're meant to be together
And nothing can keep us apart

Home
By Tara Khnanisho
25 years old

I abandoned you a long time ago
And ever since I never looked back

I was too young to care or know
We just weren't on the same track

I saw nothing but tears and pain
From the first moment I laid eyes on you

Felt like I had more to lose than gain
I decided I didn't want to think it through

I'm sorry to see you unhappy
So lifeless, for you I pray

It's nothing less than a tragedy
To watch you slip away

Sometime I want to run back to you
And say my last goodbye

But I'm afraid to show you weakness
Because I will break down and cry

Home is where the heart is
Or at least that's what they say

My home won't be here tomorrow
Because you are already gone today

6.

Youth Issues I

*The first person we learned to hate
was ourselves. Heads bent down as we
walked past the mirror of shame
comparing shapes of man and woman*
—Alanna Garavaglia

Dave Zirin: There are some pretty heavy issues explored in this section. Do you think young people today have more complicated issues to deal with the generations before them?

Etan Thomas: It sure seems that way. Even though the older generation always says nothing is new under the sun, I think young people are being exposed to things at a younger age.

Dave Zirin: What inspired your poem on the CD, "The Trap," and what do you hope young readers take away from it?

Etan Thomas: One of the major issues I have seen, especially when speaking to young boys, is the fact that they all want to be in the NBA or NFL, or be some type of professional athlete. They don't realize how difficult a goal that is to attain, and how putting all of their eggs in that one basket can be setting themselves up for failure. Young people have to realize that they can go after whatever dream they desire, but just in case things don't work out according to plan, it's always good to have a plan B.

Dave Zirin: What inspired your poem that follows, "Hip Hop"?

Etan Thomas: On one hand I was defending a culture that I grew up on and respect while at the same time challenging that same culture to be more positive, uplifting and empowering as it shapes the minds of our youth.

Hip Hop
By Etan Thomas

I have listened to Rakim on a rocky mountaintop and yes I've heard hip hop
Extracted positivity from an abundance of negative aspects that have been flashing
      across my TV screen
Blasted into the eardrums of the mainstream
Trickling down often seen catastrophes as realities from sea to shining sea
Kweli sentenced me to reside captive in lyrical institutions
While Digable Planets mellowed my mind
Public Enemy reminded me of revolution
And Dead Prez quickly followed in line
A tribe on a quest for knowledge

You speak in many tongues
Some native others foreign to my eardrum
I hear your versatility
Even if it doesn't apply to me
I can appreciate your creativity
But you're capable of so much more
What is your source of motivation?
Tangled in the ancient chain of greed money and profit
Three evils working hand and hand to destroy mentalities with a serpent's tongue
The gatekeeper to the minds of our young
You shape and form personalities like clay

I've seen what she can be
Infinite potential able to be reached without a quantum's leap
Positivity is lying on the sand washed ashore
Moments from drowning
Impatiently awaiting the alarm to sound
Rescue missions were supposed to be sent in droves to revive her soul
She's gasping for polluted air to fill her lungs with diluted thoughts
Contaminated creations hovering over the atmosphere like smog
You can easily view environmental hazards that should matter most

Melting glaciers should raise flags of future plans
of tattered dreams and shattered hopes
Climate change driven by greenhouse gases that poison our once clean air
Nobody pays attention
The fog of clouded language has mangled our previously pure atmosphere
It has destroyed one of God's creations through the enhancement of technological
     innovations
A temperature changing at a rate faster than ever
And now we're seeing the consequences of our actions manufactured in warmed
     polar caps
But it's still not enough to warrant a change
Positivity is beautiful when it's at its best
Manifesting reinventions of awareness should come quickly
Before she has taken her last breath

Common used to love her but I still care for her dearly
She has become fluent in speaking the language of infidelity
She's forgotten her vows
Discarded her commitment to uplifting my spirit
Our connection has dwindled to an occasional touch
The quiet whisper of a Black Thought in the moonlight still speaks to me in volumes
Sending rays of Nas, Lupe Fiasco and Mos Def to shine through the cracks of my
     barely opened window
Slum Village Joe Buddens and Lil Brother can't smother the multitudes as they do
     for me for they are few and far between
Monogamy has never been your reality
I exist as one of your many concubines who you refuse to adequate sample time for
You adapt to many forms
A chameleon type transformation
As I am left alone
Wondering when you will return to me

Hip hop
A reflection of the society that birthed it
Nurturing thoughts of belonging to a stolen identity
Created means of expression

But you can't blame hip hop
When societal ills spills across the pages of your reality
You can't point the finger at hip hop
When out of work comics go on racist rants at the laugh factory
You can't blame hip hop
When Mel Gibson spews racial epithets on taped conversations
You can't blame hip hop
When Don Imus degrades black women in a national setting
You can't turn to hip hop with an accusatory finger pointing out the need to censor

You wanna rid the country of a society that has been here for years
Deportation proceedings
Denunciation
Protest rights to live civilly as undeserved amnesty
You would rather simply prosper off the talents without accepting the multitude in
        your reality
Devoted to securing a border to ward off unwanted guests
Apparently perceived as a troublesome mess
Adding to the stress of everyday life
Wasting taxpayers' dollars on the multitudes that don't bother to speak the king's
        language anyway
Impulsive
Negative aspects seen as outnumbered masses regardless of concrete data
A written reality you want to edit
Cut and paste into fiction
Border control seen as a method of self defense
Objections thrown as a patriotic duty to the continuing of our future
Or so it seems
There is nothing more negligent than attempting to address the problems one
        finds on a branch by censoring the leaves

Lost

By Naliyah Kaya

25 years old

I'm tired of these
Low self-esteem havin, back stabbin, boyfriend grabbin, simple minded females!
Running off at the mouth
Always talking about something they know nothing about
Criticizing, complaining, blaming everyone . . . but themselves
So concerned with monetary wealth and you wonder why we have a hard time getting
     respect from men?
It starts with self

You steppin out in your "sexy" attire, wearing nothing more than stilettos and
     some flimsy piece of see-through cloth capitalistically passed off as a two
     hundred dollar designer dress
And by the way
Why the hell doesn't it cover your breast?
I'm just sayin
You look this way everywhere you go
And you wonder why men refer to you as a ho?

Acrylic nails, synthetic hair, contact colored eyes, plastic nose, push up bra,
     painted face, tatted design on your barely covered behind
And you're mad because he isn't interested in your mind?

With all that fast talkin and switch walkin
Your mentality deserted dignity long ago when you started bouncin on the center
     between his thighs
The result?
A hardened heart and dagger eyes
A vindictive tongue and a mouth that flows with malicious words
Spitting them on others every chance you get
Sometimes swallowing but . . .
No harm done because you've already been infected

I know I know
It's because you have always felt neglected
Daddy wasn't there
Not to mention Mommy was workin
Not enough attention
So you're just reacting to rejection
But you're grown now
So we can drop the excuses for a second and be real about this
It's about more than cars, jewelry, sex, clothes and who you know
It's about remembering Who You Are

They Call Her Exotic…
By Naliyah Kaya
25 years old

Once seen as an oddity,
constantly exploited sexually
Judged from the color and shape of her eyes to the volume and curvature of her
        breast 'n' thighs
Critiqued on the size of her derriere and the texture 'n' length of her hair
Idealized measurements—unrealistic
Living amongst various standards of beauty,
none of which reflects what the mirror does

She moves to a rhythm all her own
Defying society as she paints it with her uncategorized beauty—
leaving heads turned, only to see remnants of her existence in the shades of nature
So natural, her body refuses to conform to male-made standards
Its curves constantly draw outside the guidelines
Eyes on fire, blazing with dreams, inscribing them upon reality
Self-conscious only in the sense of knowing self
Often equated with erotic, but she's so sen-su-al
To them, a pleasing vision for men is her sole purpose
They fail to recognize the tenacity which drives this woman of mighty strength
Her lips carved a need for the term *articulate*

Mind so strikingly intelligent
Mentality blindingly beautiful—
refuses to be subservient!
She is not one to follow BUT TO BE FOLLOWED
Her insight drips with passion,
spilling on the young who feverishly collect knowledge—
aspiring to touch her wisdom
reaching to grasp her joy—
Autonomy unparalleled able to pass through time,
realizing a need for connection but not to any individual
Grounded in Faith, cared for by Common Sense and propelled by Hope
She is the essence dreams are made from
Enticing others to believe the unattainable can be a reality
She embodies Dignity and Resilience—
who emanates in her evolution,
refusing to be tied to old ways when revelations emerge
She cannot be confined to convention
—Queen of reinvention—
Unafraid to defy norms,
Her thoughts insinuate revolution—
actions bringing forth solution
She is the Answer
Indefinable, yet constantly redefined

She responds to but ONE name . . .

Authentic

Beautiful Women, for All the Lost Souls
By Alanna Garavaglia
18 years old

The first person we learned to hate
was ourselves. Heads bent down as we
walked past the mirror of shame
comparing shapes of man and woman,
neglecting our children,
too afraid to raise female and interracial generations.

The most powerful form of control
started with dividing, conquering,
old against young,
men against women,
white against black,
you against the world . . .
but God, a man,
came up with this "perfect" plan—
this paradise called life.
We breathe oxy for moron.
Start with the women
and rape them
until one woman
stops depending on someone other than herself
to save her.
Divide her against her self
that the man showed her to destroy.
Keep her on the edge of layers
so society doesn't guess the dirty little secrets
resting inside of a woman's breast.
And what's more to come,
when the truth comes out,
man will still get the upper hand,
because he is better
than the body he came from,
because of the penis,
the extra bread he eats,
the extra hours he gets,
he learns it's destiny
because in society,
he has the strength of the
Almighty.
The skin I'm in.
He's inherited his skin by a
divine man who created paradise by
the heart, mind, body and spirit

of a woman.
Full length debates on whether or not
Joan was strong and powerful to
conquer men. Why was it so hard to
believe that women and their tones are great things?
They got James Davis from
The Gathering Storm to play the part
of Juliet.
My genes are beautiful
and they protect me against male ego.
You will never fully understand
the power of Athena and Aphrodite
because of the characteristics of Ares,
shed beneath his skin.
Many men see women as diluted
versions of the original man, and some
women succumb to that belief—
turning it into a language man only
understands.
You take what you are given
and if you are not given anything,
you take it another way.
The divide has been successful because you
bark down the back of your own mother,
her heart suffocating—
the same woman who bore sweat,
blood and pain.
She dances in a video and grinds
for money, because that's seen as
the only standard of use.
Natural beauty hidden by makeup,
ass up and breasts out
as if that's her only occupation.
Her only standard of dignity.
What about that pride?
Skeptical of raising a daughter because

of the society we live in,
where people like you still appraise
beauty and humanity,
strength and power,
of going someplace and doing something
with your life off of whether you are an X or Y chromosome.
My mind is potent,
my heart is a storm,
my beauty is down deep,
my soul is uplifting,
and I
and every woman like me
are inspiring—aspiring.
We are blueprints for what
your mothers used to be,
before the rapes
and the dilution to what we're
supposed to be.
Under bright aura is substance,
history and wealth,
so when you place
women in a category beneath yourself,
you are only lowering yourself.
Hate is equal.

Ape
By Darius Emmanuel
13 years old

Sometimes you need an alias or an alter ego—
A little bit of evil to put up for the people
I call mine Ape
and Ape like from the matrix just murdered Morpheous
then killed Keanu Reeves with no intent to follow ordinances
I'm more of a dormant abhorrence
If I'm so horrible, then how does this verse sound glorious?

Ape is curious George with a satchel and a sword in it,
wondering if offing himself would be worth it
so imperfect all he needs is rhymes and verses
stranger to himself—that's why he speaks in third person
Live life like he is dark road turnin', swervin'
Silly from Irish bourbon, screamin' at drivers cursin'
and every once in a while stops at a curb to steal pedestrian purses:
Coach, Louis, Ermis Burkin . . .
Recklessness
Negative
No tangible evidence
of this kid having ever been more than a detriment
so I start taking detours in my verses
replace the curses
and of course in the midst of it all ask myself
Why is life worth it?
I never really liked proverbs and idioms but
Life is like an ill mannered clerk behind the counter
and when life hands you lemons
Take a knife
cut it into fives and squeeze the citrus in your eyes
to hope you become blind and can't see your own demise but
to find the truth you must first point out the lies
and the truth is . . .
I'm gonna get off this stage
You're gonna forget this piece
and less importantly . . . you're gonna forget me
I'm gonna smile, crack a joke, and act as if I hadn't said a thing when in all reality
        I saw you shift in your seat
Because you probably knew Ape,
Yet you didn't know . . . me.

The Box

By Marlon Ampree

22 years old

The box is what raises him
Too young to go out on his own, so he watches the box
When he comes home from school he watches it because that is all he can do
He neglects his homework, puts it to the side
No mother at home to guide his free time
She is at her third job
So he prepares his seat and watches
His favorite shows have no ratings
The information infiltrates his iris
No SpongeBob
Instead his head he bobs as it becomes a sponge and the visions are water
Absorbing all the material until the mind is soaked
He watches all the programming that will eventually program him
He watches the violent episodes of terror
There is no respect for human life so he loses respect for his own
He watches the crime the news always talks about
No father in the home but plenty of black men fill his box
The black faces he relates to, the men in the box become his role models
They have no 9 to 5
Instead their actions could get 5 to 9
They tote weapons and call women everything but women
They brag about having money and disregard education
So he continues neglecting his
They promote promiscuity
So he plans on having relations instead of relationships
The language is definitely for adult ears
So at such a tender age he uses such coarse language
But this box isn't a onetime occurrence, it consumes him every day, every night
He spends more time with the box than anything else
He watches and determines his profession

Because of these people's actions he decides he wants to act on either cocaine or heroin

The rich blacks in his box are either drug dealers or former drug dealers
Oh but I can't forget the athletes in the box
He sometime watches the ball games in the box
He watches them play but would rather do what the dealers do
See the dealers in the box acquire money faster than any other profession in the box
The money can buy him the things he sees in the box
He wants the designer labels that are put in his face
Instead of securing his future he is determined to secure new things
When he sleeps sounds from the box still enter his ears and they seep into his mind
The visions he previously watched then dominate his dreams
The box is now determining his direction
Instead of play he would rather watch the box
There is no off button on his box, it stays on
And his mother, the job she always stays on
So those lights will always stay on
His mother is a strong woman but he never sees her
He only sees the women in the box
Selling themselves as objects
So he now accepts them as objects
And no one is home to object
He wipes the box's glass so he can see the images clearly
But no matter how much he cleans the images still show distorted
This box is not a computer screen
This box is not a television
Instead it's real visions
The box is a window, from its pane he watches the world's pains
While through media bad things are reinforced
It's the real world that is the strongest force
We blame entertainment for society's ills but it's society that is ill
See, the village should raise the child but what happens when the village has
        become vile
We are upset about how we are presented on reality TV
But what about reality
What about poverty,
What about disease,
See, art imitates life not the other way around

Yet we tryna fix our problems the other way around
We want less flavor of love and more Cosby
But when we going to realize Cosby isn't what caused me
It was a village and a family
So I, no we, need to fix the boy's box
Because unlike TV, eventually, he will do more than just watch

Falling Down (When I Grow Up . . .)
By Kira
13 years old

The clock strikes once again, and I remember that decisions must soon be made.
"Life is short," they always say, but the public never said, "Life can seem long."
My fingers acknowledge the table beneath them, for it is my only shield.
"I need more time," I could lie. My fingers would pace even faster than before.
The clock again strikes, this time with an open-ended sound, as if to say, "Eternity
        is to follow."
But I break this metal hold around me by proclaiming, "I shall live in the moment."
What moment? The moment to come. The moment now. The moment before.
Ask me no more questions. I know who I am. I know what I will be.
How? I am what I decide to do, decide to answer, decide to respond to in the
        moment.
I will let your fists drive down fast upon the table, as my fingers' beat starts to fade.
I will let your eyes shut, as mine begin to open.
All you need—and all I need—to do is stop making holes. As we do this, we won't
        fall down, and the clock won't strike.
We will finally know how to answer our questions, if we just think.
And yet, as I say this, my fingers begin to hit the table again.
Alas, I finally decode its reasoning. For this time, it is different.
I am not afraid. I am just concentrating, I am just living today. Living now.

Food for Thought

By Danny Crawford

26 years old

Lord give me the strength
Not to go back in these streets
Please help me find an alternative
Because even dogs gotta eat
I been home 92 days
Spent 15 years in a cage
Then they put me back in society
And say, "you better behave"
With no education
And a criminal record
I never even got a first chance
So a second isn't expected
I was locked up for selling drugs
Got caught with a couple of bags
But instead of sending me to jail
They should've made me volunteer at a rehab
There's other alternatives
To incarceration
Because the road the government is taking
My people won't make it
I'm not rehabilitated
More like humiliated
I'm not guilty your honor
Let's just say I'm affiliated
Because who really made it?
How was crack created?
My project is infested
It needs to be fumigated
Okay now let me break it down for you
On how this game is played
Let's compare it to a deck of cards
And the government is the ace of spades

They make deals with other countries
To supply those things
Then they turn around and sell it to them Kings
Now the King-pin takes the work
The government wiped they hands clean
Now it gets distributed to the jacks and queens
Those are the guys you see
Running the corners
The workers are the deuces thru 10
It's in that order
It's the perfect setup and we all are caught up
The government controls it all from the prisons to the borders

Purple Hearts for Prostitutes
By Taylor Cooper
20 years old

Ladies of the night are in the trenches of war

They line bedspreads with the hate, lust, greed and desires of the world and battle
        to make someone proud . . . of their skills

From her hips to her lips
tips of her fingers to the tip of her tongue
the moistness in her throat to the moistness between her thighs
she is a weapon
built and used for the art of war
the war of sex
sex without meaning
so death without meaning
like so many pointless wars

They are soldiers
fighting for ideas and concepts and feelings
that should already be theirs

like acceptance, like self worth

Whores have one of the hardest occupations on earth
one of the few you could get arrested for
as if trying to love away somebody else's hurt and pain
could ever be compared to theft and murder

Women who devoted their nights to being what you want
and their days to not knowing who they are
and the only way she knows how to change things is to go back to the
trenches of the bed sheets

Lie with the enemy, have her foxhole intruded
drowning out the sounds of her tears with the sounds of her moans
the sounds of planes flying with the sounds of gunshots

They fight for women whose job this ISN'T
for those that have had it confirmed by men that only their body is what they re-
quire, desirable as they might be, love and trust and faith are not needed
in times of war
and these girls pay the price with their souls trying to love away their solitude

Prostitutes fight for the American Dream harder than anyone else
after all
selling dope doesn't chip away at your soul
if you're not a user
Imagine revolutionaries cuffed and tied in the back of police cars
while these girls are cuffed and tied to bed and chairs
while playing cops and robbers
better yet
while playing cop and prisoner
better yet
playing hostage situation

It's really all for the cause
and in the pause of position changes

and being called back overseas
she is the only one to admit her flaws

She is as real as it gets because
men will always sell shoes
before PlayStations
before TVs
before haircuts
before drugs
before ever thinking it was possible to consider their bodies

These women, they in the trenches on extended tours for freedom
the freedom of girls who are traded into this war
Those kidnapped, drugged and sold in France, Japan, and California
For those forced to fight with less means than her

And if she ever conceives anything other than
the lies and desires men pay her for
the envy of other women who don't understand her struggle
conceives anything other than
the disapproval of the church
the whispers of indecent words
and loud stares from down the street
conceives more than
the tight clothes she wears not to
show off her "training"
but to bandage her wounds and scars

If she ever conceives children
when they are old enough to understand
the concepts of pain and love
acceptance and self worth

She will tell them

"Mommy . . . is a soldier"

Remember the Two

By Brandy Stoner

24 years old

I will always remember the two. I remember because my brothers were so tormented at their own high school, where most of my middle school and elementary school tormenters ended up attending. I remember because I have a friend who was living in Littleton but attending another Denver school, and she would be scarred by the memories herself if not for fate. I remember because so many of my friends wore dark trench coats and were fascinated with weapons, and with music and books that gave words to the pain that they only knew how to express through aggression.

I always had my words. I was accepted to a magnet school, and I left behind my bullies. Through an unspoken pact with the other kids who were leaving the same school, we would quietly reinvent ourselves and not tell anyone at the new school what incredible outcasts we really were.

But.

I told my mother, before receiving the acceptance letter for the school for the gifted, that I would rather kill myself than attend my current school another year. Months later, when she saw the shock on my face as I read the letter, Mom looked at me with wet lashes and comforted, "Oh, Brandy. I'm so sorry." Bewildered, I looked up at her and said, "Why? I got in." We were both relieved.

I watched the newscasts seven years later with tears running down my neck, not just for the 13 victims, but for the victims who became aggressors. I just kept thinking, "There but for the grace of God go I." Even now, when talk of the deaths arises anew each spring, fellow former outcasts and I—who are otherwise strangers—momentarily share what Eudora Welty called "age group looks."

Besides grace, though, I had advantages that the bullied boys of Columbine High did not.

Taunts ranged from "K-Mart, K-Mart is our store! We shop there 'cause we are poor!" to "Brainy's got a gun, and she's come undone." We didn't shop at K-Mart. Frankly, in a one-income working-class home with five children, K-Mart was a little upscale. Financial advantage was not mine. I certainly couldn't afford therapy. We were happy to have occasional dental care. But I had a mother who was surprisingly sympathetic to my adolescent isolation, and who grasped the concept of a "teachable moment" before that became a catchphrase.

I once explained the plight of a fellow eighth-grade classmate to my mother: "Ryan is pretty weird, Mom. He tells people sometimes that I am going to be his girlfriend. Just because I am nice to him. Do you know why I am nice to him, Mom?

Because I keep thinking that one day he is going to get sick of how mean everyone is to him, and he will snap, and come back to kill us all, and I am hoping he will remember I was nice to him, and spare me. I don't want to be his girlfriend, but I don't want him to kill me someday either." It was a bizarre statement, and Mom and I had a good, awkward laugh before I made my own confession.

"Um, Mom? You know why I worry that Ryan is going to flip out someday? Because when they say 'Brainy's got a gun,' and laugh . . . sometimes . . . I think about it. How good it would feel, just to shut them up. I don't really want to hurt anyone. I just want them to stop."

Mom sat in silence while I cried into my folded arms and onto the kitchen table and my algebra textbook. Then she said, "I can see why you would feel that way." She went on to tell me that she knows I am frustrated, and that she would like to tell me that there was a magic bullet, made of lead or otherwise, that would make them stop. But there wasn't. And there would not be one anytime soon.

The scant hope she offered was that I had potential they didn't have, despite every material advantage, and that while one day I would be secure and happy and still smarter than they were, my tormentors would struggle with insecurity and entitlement the whole of their lives. That being said, for the duration of our wait for the ultra-competitive magnet school's response, she and my father began looking to purchase a home in another school district. I was privileged with parents who recognized the difference between genuine despair and average adolescent angst. I had parents who would move all of their children to save one. We were taught to cast aside our differences in desperate times—"All for one and one for all." I was born with enough intelligence and talent that my education did not hinge on my parents' following the proverbial Joneses into what for me would have been a suburban hell of conformity and mediocrity.

I do not claim to know whether "the two" had parents who were emotionally removed from their children. It is not fair to surmise about the parents, yet hundreds of assumptions are made about their boys. As a parent myself though, I think it is fair to say that if our children are stockpiling weapons, and we do not take notice, we have become too far removed from their lives. I do know that I count myself blessed that I have a mother who I could beg the question, "How do I make them stop?" and who would offer the response, "How do you make you stronger than your misery and better than their barbs?"

And so I remember them today. Not by name, not by the infamy that they felt would make them legendary, but as two scared and scarred adolescents. I remembered them eight years ago, when one of my brothers opted for home tutoring rather than enduring any more socially based shame.

I remembered them three years ago, when my kindergartner cried because a girl she thought was her friend tied the shoelaces on her brand-new pink Chucks to the jungle gym, and the laces had to be cut at the end of recess. I remembered them last year, when my daughter quickly became part of the A-group at her new elementary school but remained kind and helpful, and the teacher said she seemed to reach out to socially and academically struggling classmates. I remembered them a few months ago, when, now in second grade, amidst an ill-founded custody battle, she told me of shoving and taunts—"Nobody cares about Tia." I remembered them when I asked her how that made her feel. Do you know what she said? "I'm sorry for whatever happened that gave him such low self-esteem. We should pray for him. But I'm not going to let him make me feel bad about myself."

I have remembered them this decade, in my parenting. We remember the two by providing our children with an "emotional vocabulary." We remember the two by talking about bullies and forgiveness and self-esteem. That way, we remember the two. We forgive the two. And we honor the lost thirteen.

Sampled Love
By Chaina N. Dobbins
21 years old

I used to love you.
Back when you were original and pure. Back when the best of you couldn't be
        recorded, adorned, packaged and stored. You know, back when you were
        sure.
In those days I could dial you up to hear your voice. But then you changed your tune.
Now I have to search archives of albums with an accompaniment just to find you.
Orchestrated sonata now the echo of a symphony.
Thunderous tenor now a feeble mezzo forte falsetto.
What happened to you?
You were a well structured sonnet and I fell in love with your lyrical design.
But you couldn't keep time. Or keep up with the times, that is. Or were too busy
        trying, I guess.
Cus as the people around you became callous and crude so did you.
When they told you chivalry was dead you listened, and shifted your stanzas to suit
        their taste.
You hastily diminished our duet with your decrescendo into delirium.
And you did it all so quickly there may be no turning back.

But while you and what once moved you may have come to a rest, no coda could
  conclude my repetition of your rhythm.
So rather than recite your requiem, I'll repeat your rhapsodies until their romantic
  notes are no longer in my register.

Survive and Advance
By Max Turner
19 years old

It was a closed casket
We tryin to keep it open
Lookin at a star
Wishin and hopin
Prayin for a way
Maybe a solution
But they angry
Out here for retribution
And these boys shootin
With automatic weapons
Out the same house
That they Momma slept in
And we steppin
Out in the finest gators
And if you disagree
We call you a hater
Sign of the times
You can ask Prince
Out here chasin dollars
We don't make sense
Living for the money
Fightin over streets
They studio gangsters
Can't die over beats
Can't trust they words
They all hypocrites

Black on black crime
Used to raise black fists
They say do or die
We say hit or miss
And they scared to talk
without they affiliates
Born on the west
Raised in the south
Somethin like the best
I do it for the damn house
These dudes all a mess
But I remain the same
Just like Kanye West
Tryin to be T-Pain
Not here to place blame
Just an explanation
They out here coonin
Like we on plantations
Assassinations
Of our community
Remember when rappers made records bout unity
But now we all hustle
And we all thugs
And our pioneers
Are makin Flava of Loves
Now the game's crazy
Suckers say it's dead
Cuz we superman hoes
And do the stanky leg
And I'm gonna play it
Long as it bumps
What's the difference between walkin it out and humpty hump
These suckers all chumps
Just some spoiled children
Cats is sensitive
All caught up in they feelings

The Mysterious Scourge
By Olajide Omojarbi
Age 24

The scourge came like a wind and now,
It has become the inhabitants of the humans.

Like the weather: everybody talks about it
But no one knows what to do about it.

It is afflicting the young and the old,
The weak and the strong,
The single and the married.

Some call it a plague from God
To reduce promiscuity among humankind.

Others say it's an ordinary disease,
That will wither away like the breath.
But alas! It hasn't.

Time ticks and death toll rises.
It had stormed Africa like a thief in the night
Stealing away ignorant souls,
Leaving the fortunate mourning their loved ones.
Discrimination and stigmatization are its children.

In an effort to curb it, solutions have been proffered:
"Say no to drugs," "Abstinence, fidelity."
The slogans are working, but on slow pace;
Slower than the snail.
It's killing the hope of our future leaders and
It's denying us our destinies.
The cure is the antidote but until then,

I'm flagging up a campaign to say

No to ignorance!
No to prejudice!
No to superstition!

Africa, let's wake up from our slumber.
Hasn't it consumed us enough?

We can't fight it by despising its affliction.
We can't stop it by spreading the virus.

We can only curb it by passing this message:
An HIV free generation is possible.
Take the lead! Spread the words!

One Day Away
By Sarah Hilware
17 years old

World AIDS Day . . . do you really think that is sufficient?
Clearly, one day to recognize this serial killer is deficient . . .
Every nine minutes, someone's quality of life is ripped away . . . dignity, dreams,
    and longevity
disappear like the stock of condoms disappear from corner stores in low-income
    neighborhoods . . .
People with PhDs, MDs, and JDs are in the woods if they think that the cure is
    medicine.
And my patience is wearing thin,
Because the real enemy is not the virus itself,
It is poverty,
Every day, it is being placed farther back on a shelf . . . second, third, fourth,
    fifth . . . behind this
so-called "war on terror" and this "recession,"

All because we have an obsession: with money and
power,
And I'm starting to think the hour of realization will never come.
I'm starting to think that isolation, segregation, moral dehydration, and a tired,
miserable nation
will never cease.
Because ONE minuscule day for AIDS cannot suffice for 33.4 million patients . . .
One day does not bring me peace.

And ONE is not a fix for the issue of sexism that is so morbidly obese.
Because our women are penetrated with this disease more than our men,
Because they have families to feed,
So they give their bodies to the hungry business of prostitution,
The institution full of pollution . . . the epitome of disparity,
And one day does not make the problem of this pandemic go away,
When that one day leaves, AIDS will stay,
The little Rwandan girl who wants to have a family one day will pray . . . that her
t-cells will get
better . . .
She will hope and wish that she had a doctor . . .
And a worried mother in Washington, DC, will write a letter to the insurance
companies, begging
for anyone to cover treatment so that her baby will be born negative,
Because ONE DAY is not enough

To bring back the sense of pride in her eyes before she contracted the virus,
One day has not retracted the hepatitis she got from her weakened immune system,

THIS IS OUR PANDEMIC.
It is not hers, or his, or theirs.
It is ours.
And one day, we must own it.
Because we are one day away from letting it own us instead.

I am Me

By Yetunde Mondie-Sapp

13 years old

I saw my reflection, yesterday,
atop the rippling water,
and wondered if other people,
see me,
how I see me?

I am deep like the sea, I am me
I wonder what heaven is like
I hear hearts beating like drums
I see what others don't
I want to make a change
I am deep like the sea, I am me

I pretend I don't care
I feel confused
I regret the words I said
I worry I take things for granted
I am sad when others cry
I am deep like the sea, I am me

I understand life is a privilege
I say "nobody's perfect" because I know I'm not
I smile when the sun shines
I dream a world of peace
I try to say goodbye
I hope for tomorrow

I am deep like the sea,
I reflect what I see,
I am weak, I am strong,
I am me

After hurricane Ivan hit Grenada I spoke at a couple of different schools in Grenada to boost everyone's spirits. Photographer: Grenadian Embassy

After a Fatherhood Panel Discussion in Harlem with Allan Houston, Etan Thomas, Amare Stoudemire, Julian Thomas, J Ivy, Chaz Shepperd, Pastor Michael Walrond, Messiah Ramkissoon, Styles P, and Chris Broussard
Photographer: Kendall Crabtree

Julian Thomas, Etan Thomas, Kim Bearden, and Ron Clarke at the Ron Clarke Academy
Photographer: J. Amezqua

DC Youth Slam Team

With legendary Amiri Baraka at a poetry event at the Blvd in Maryland
Photographer: Carlisle Sealy

Speaking to a group of kids at my high school, Booker T. Washington, in Tulsa, Oklahoma
Photographer: Carlisle Sealy

After speaking to a group of small children at the YMCA
Photographer: Albert Nimley

With my family: wife Nichole, Malcolm, Imani, and baby Sierra. Photographer: Kendall Crabtree

Speaking at Prince George's Correctional Facility. Photographer: Carlisle Sealy

With Malcolm Shabazz, J Ivy, Julian Thomas, Abiodun Oyewole of The Last Poets, and Messiah Ramkissoon at a Fatherhood Panel at Crenshaw East Church in Manhattan. Photographer: Kendall Crabtree

With Trey Songz and Kal Penn before a rally in Chicago. Photographer: Alexys Feaster

With my manager Carlisle Sealy in front of the capitol

With Rev. Yearwood, Maino, and T.I. after speaking at a Respect My Vote event in DC. Photographer: Carlisle Sealy

With Malcolm, taking a stand for Trayvon Martin. Photographer: Nichole Thomas

7.
Youth Issues II

*The plus size woman doesn't need Howard Stern
and his infinite wisdom, to let her know that she is
overweight. She is greeted by that daunting reality each
morning as she showers and dresses herself*

—Nikeya Greene

Dave Zirin: These again are some pretty heavy issues. Do you ever think that these issues are too heavy?

Etan Thomas: Too heavy? No, because they are real. These are the issues that are on the minds of young people. I didn't ask them to specifically write on these topics in this section. I just labeled the section "Youth Issues." Some of the other sections had more specific titles, but this content came directly from them. These are the issues they are concerned with and want to be able to share with the world. In this section, you'll read poems from young minds that range from societal treatment of plus-size women, to violence, to young people throwing their lives away, to depression, to glass ceilings in the workplace.

Dave Zirin: Would you ever have an issue presenting a piece that you didn't agree with?

Etan Thomas: Definitely not. I appreciate the passion and creativity of the poets. Different political issues tend to dominate the conversation whenever I speak at schools. I always want to hear their positions. I like when they have an opinion that differs from mine and we can have a debate, or they engage in a debate amongst themselves. I think hearing different perspectives is always helpful. I want them to think and present their ideas and beliefs. That's the whole point of this project.

Dave Zirin: What was the inspiration for your poem "Voting"?

Etan Thomas: Before President Obama electrified the youth in the 2008 election, many young people refrained from exercising their right to vote. It would always frustrate me when, after having a wonderful conversation or debate with a young person, I'd discover that they had no interest in actually voting whether they were of age or not. Many young people simply failed to see the point or need to actually vote. I wrote this poem particularly for them.

Voting
By Etan Thomas

How could you not cast your vote?
How could you cope with the problems of present-day society knowing that you
      went quietly?
Silence has always been the sworn enemy of democracy

Unwilling to lend your voice to whatever cause you believe in
You're deceiving yourself if you think your vote doesn't matter
Much more than idle chatter in soundless corners within the borders of your
      confinement
You've assigned yourself to a muzzled opinion
Sending your ability to actually make a difference into an abyss of hopelessness
I know you're not comfortable with the overall situation we're standing in
So why don't your actions follow suit
Frozen in time like a mannequin
Unable to move for progress

Your muted passions go unaccounted for
As your choice to remain captive to voiceless patterns hampers your source of strength

You keep your voice concealed like a weapon
Loaded with the power to shower opposing forces with automatic clips of influence
Your true strength remains in its holster
See, talk is cheap
The truth creeps into reality no matter how much noise you bellow
The fastest draw in the west you're not
Back in the day they would have called you yellow
Screaming it from the mountaintops above

Or maybe simply a disgrace
Like going from the pride of public enemy to the flavor of love
You should be embarrassed
Casting a vote is a gift you should cherish

You have mountains of opinions that send your emotions into volcanic eruptions
Your productions of contempt for political corruption wrestle with your serenity
How could the essence of your tranquility possibly be at peace in a time of war?
Your personal core beliefs that you would be willing to fight for
Soaring to heights of desired plights
Your desires for this country to truly be all it can be
You want to protect the investment of your livelihood
Your rights trampled by hooded cowboys disguised as politicians
Disgust with their unreliability creates a barricade of a distrusting mentality
An obstruction of justice formed into a mountain-sized barrier
You've grown tired of hearing them promise to always deliver like a UPS carrier

They've missed your train of thought
Frustration has fought battles with your trust in the system
Voices dismissed as meaningless
Deemed irrelevant like Katrina victims
A script that is played on a continuous reel
Your rights carefully taken away piece by piece like a banana peel
But what are you doing to change history's pattern?
You're cheating the game like Parcell and Donaghy
You want progress to go fast like Lightning McQueen
But you never felt moved to go to a booth?
Hollowed dreams rotted like tooth decay
But you stay away from casting a vote?
If you think that things can't get worse if you don't vote again
Then you have a vivid imagination like a backyardigan

Who told you that your vote doesn't matter?
The history of our battered grandparents
The people before us that fought for our right to cast our ballot
They were met with violence

They wanted to silence our voice
Take the choice from our grasp
Transform us into one unaccounted-for mass
Pass us off as invisible

Have you forgotten the suffrage movement?
Or are you choosing to ignore the scores of battles that rattled views of a woman's
        proper place
Silent in the home without a face in politics
The race to equality
A slow-paced hard-fought fight for equal opportunity

Women were given the right to vote in the 1920s
But 40 years later access to people who looked like me was still denied
The sixties weren't that long ago
Not given the right until 1965
Do you remember Edmund Pettis Bridge?
Where Alabama state troopers brutally clubbed peaceful marchers crossing the
        bridge on their way to Montgomery to demand voting rights
Go and google the term Bloody Sunday
Read how Governor George Wallace instructed law enforcement to assault, dispel,
        and harass peaceful demonstrators with billy clubs bull whips and tear gas
See images of pigs mounted on horseback attacking people with maximum force
        for wanting to cast a vote

You owe them more
Than to sit there and not exercise a right that they died fighting for
Blood sweat and tears through years of suffering
Trying to exist in the midst of opposition that met them with the force of an army
        while law enforcement turned a blind eye
Or joined in the fight for the opposing side
Could you imagine living in that time?
It's a crime we should never forget
A past that legally lynched our people with a red white and blue rope
You think about that
Next time you decide not to cast your vote

127

Spit for Change
By Daryl Fortson

20 years old

We spit for change when the change don't come. Cuz the change won't come without change so we must alter the frame in which we frame our thoughts, therefore changing the thoughts within it. We spit for change, for our own standard of beauty, for the cutie in the back of the room who assumes and speaks doom upon her for what she sees in the mirror is not the acceptable scene in the teen magazines. I'm here to tell you we're queens, so raise those chocolate eyes to the bluest skies instead of compromising your God-given mind, brainwashed to ask for them bluest eyes. Don't be afraid of the change you bring, for with each confident breath your own freedom will ring. I say sistas, reach for the prize of self worth, self respect, self love. Spit that change, watch your world change, and you will overcome.

Revolution
By Keisha A. Mitchell

20 years old

If you love the revolution put your hands up.
Said if you're down for Black people keep your hands up.
    That's whatsup.
A revolution is defined as nothing more than a complete cycle,
360 degress bringing that which spins back to its start.
Cyclical with no beginning or end
the cycle demonstrating no upward or downward trends
it just is what it is.
what it always will be . . .
what is always has been . . .
Cuz most of these so called revoultionaries can tell you all the names and dates of
        black notables and necessaries
crucial to the advancement of black history but have failed to educate themselves
        on facts that most would consider elementary.
Like the fact that
Tigers don't live in Africa
and Igloos don't exist

and just because you look a certain way doesn't mean thats what you represent
but
these rebel leaders of the new school are fascinated with old news and try to follow
        in the footsteps of idols who most
of us glamorize in hindsight but in their day, were no more perfect than you or I
yet we glorify snippets of their lives without ever giving it a second look
Cuz out here, all it takes to be great is to spit a couple of hot lines from behind a
        podium
But in the truth's wake,
everyone would know that our favorite revolutionaries had sideline hoes,
snorted s%$# through their nose
had obsessions with the obscene
and did unmentionable things in the unseen
so you tell me,
what again makes a revolutionary?
Cuz this conscious s%$# is trendy (like the time I was nine and just had to have a
        tamoghitichi)
I said this conscious s%$# is easy,
all you have to do is go to your local college coffee shop and hear the black collec-
        tive spit for free
But from the stage to the streets is where you find the hypocrisy
cuz while the African kings pledge the conscious creed,
they still prowl brick-laid pathways for freaks crowned with weave,
close out late night festivities the morning after and call their natural black queens
        to tell them it's them they want to help bear their seeds
They got the same respect for a black woman as a little Wayne or Jeezy
but instead of hoe or bitch, insert sister or queen
and some use goals, and others use poems, and others use all the black conspiracies
        they know,
but they all pimp.
Using their blessings with words as weapons of mass deception.
Pillaging the fields sown by lies and then watered by thighs.
But
these men aren't the only ones to blame for making conciousness lame.
Cuz these women are equally blinded,
their inequities are equally binding
cuz while the "conciousness kings" secretly chase video vixens, these "concious

129

queens" are out here making mainstream wet dreams with . . . each other
they also smoke more weed, and drink more liquor than their "natural" black
   brothers
and this is who the revolution is supposed to call mother?
Please.
What yall call "conciousness" I call that other
cuz we all watch t.v.
So if you looking down at your brother or sister for wearing a fade or weave, just
   remember that B.E.T is equally as responsible for supplying the masses
   with their image of black beauty as Spike Lee is for supplying you with
   your image of conciousness, and that's just nonsense.
Cuz everything you think you know . . . well, I guess the producers told you so. But
   hey, when you're a fighter in the revolution I guess that's how it goes.
So,
If you love the revolution put your hands up.
Said if you're down for Black people keep your hands up.
That's whatsup. Just remember:
A revolution is a complete cycle.
360 degrees bringing that which spins back to its start.
Cyclical with no beginning or end,
the cycle demonstrating no upward or downward trends
it just is what it is.
What it always will be.
What it always has been.
So ask yourself (the next time you claim to be revolutionary):
Are you fighting to free the Black race? Or are you really just fighting to keep us all
   in the same place?

Society
By Kaila Trimble
17 years old

Yesterday I lived in a society where we were mostly divided
Today I want to live in a world where we are mostly united
And because we have a president who ignited the short sighted economy

Inviting the uninvited cited his references with the demographic stopped all
         vehicle traffic to answer the unrequited that
We can lead healthy lives living united
As I watch you chew my words like bubble gum
I am speaking for those whose voices aren't as high
For those whose potential education has been brought to a minimum
For those whose income stability will become deceased if taxes increase
We need the support from the elders united
Encouragement from our country undivided
Improvements from the 21st generation whose factual performance has become
         silenced
But I question
How can we unite the nation
If we cannot unite our states
How can we unite our states
If we cannot form an alliance amongst our communities
How can we unite with the community
If we cannot collectively assemble agreements with our family
How can we collectively assemble agreements with family
If each of us cannot first consolidate our anatomy
Think about it
Peace

Epitome of Success
By Aaron Small
16 years old

I stand tall and I place myself on a pedestal.
I leave seeds behind as to make a mark that will never be erased.
I want to be part of a legacy that spawned with Sam Cooke and led to the genius of
         Dr. Martin Luther King.
It's funny how everyone wants my name beside an X like Malcolm, but I can't
         seem to fathom the idea that people would cheat me out of my success.
But what is the epitome of success? We all want to be like the next one, like
         Mike/Kobe, or Usher/Drake. Now I'm not saying there's anything wrong

with that, just when will you realize that everything is never what it seems? Will that be the day that somebody calls you fake? There was a time where nobody had to worry about crimes, you see everybody was on the grind or on the front lines trying to bring America into an up rise. . But we the people have now turned into I the individual. So can we rekindle the flame and like the phoenix out of ashes claim our name, America the Beautiful? What are we fighting for? I know it's not the colors that we try to rep in our back pocket. It has to be something more. Something along the lines of, I only have 50 dollars to my name and I'm not sure what's in store. Or the fact that my kids don't have insurance and God knows I don't want them to worry anymore. With that being said, what are waiting for? We can't just sit back and watch life pass us by. When it's all said and done, you'll only be remembered by the legacy that was left behind. We give, we take, we live, but most importantly we teach. Success only comes in perfect harmony.

I Didn't Take Their Keys
By Madelaine
18 years old

Author's Note: This poem is based on a lecture I heard about drunk driving, not
from experience.
Captured in the drunkard's spell:
They're possessed by the taste
So bitter, like a cranberry
Yet so sweet, the tang sending shivers of ease down their spines
They're soon seeing double, triple—tripping over their words,
Their feet.

It's an appalling celebration, a gathering
Of those intoxicated with drink
They do stupid things, but in a way it's funny—
But I know I shouldn't laugh, so I don't—
Fantasy becomes reality in foul means
They dance and sing to a drunken ballad

Slurring music and words
With the graceful flavor of crimson
And the sparkle of a glass.

But as soon as they pick up those keys,
I can hear the squeal of tires, the scream of the sirens
The beeping of machines, the squeaking of hospital beds—my mind is screaming:
Take the keys away or else.
But I stubbornly ignore it, caught up in the fun of their drunken bliss.

It begins normal enough,
The key in the ignition, the engine thundering to life
And we back up smoothly, the headlights giving a clear view of the road
Seems a quiet night, not a sound . . .
Pretty soon, we're speeding
Laughing, joking, having too much fun
But then, as we descend another hill, headlights come into view
We swerve the wrong way trying to avoid it, and we hit the vehicle
The laughter turns to screams as the windshield shatters
I close my eyes . . .
Oh God what have I done?
The airbags inflate and I'm flung against one, with no sense of what's going on,
I'm scared and I can't do anything about it,
So I try to stay calm, trying to focus on regulating my breathing
Or listening to my pounding heart, knowing I'm still here,
And that I'm paying the price.

I shove the airbag back; it's speckled with red
I'm bleeding from cuts and my limbs are shaking
But I'm not cold.
What the hell is gong on?
The next thing I know, I'm sitting up
I can't think clearly, I'm wondering where I am
Still glad I didn't have a drink
Everything is white and everything is clean
I'm in a gown, and bandaged, an intravenous is stuck in my hand

Clear liquid dripping down from a bag above my head.

Then it hits me:

I'm in a hospital.

I'm alive.

My fuzzy mind hears distant, soft voices and it all comes back to me:

The drinks—I should have known better than to let them drink in the first place.

Getting into the car,

Crashing . . .

Blacking out from the shock.

My parents come in then, their faces showing many emotions:

Disbelief, sadness, anger, and, most of all, utter relief

I open my mouth and nothing comes out, only a squeak.

What happened?

I want to know where my friends are so badly

Were they in the beds next to me?

Were they in different wards?

The weird thing is, I already had a feeling where they've gone

I'm glad to be alive—

That's what makes me feel guilty and sick.

Mom sits on the bed, takes my hand, and says the words I've been dreading to hear:

"Your friends . . . I'm sorry . . . but they're gone."

Her voice chokes up and she hugs me, just glad that I'm okay

But I'm so broken, so confused.

I can only cry, the tears hot against my skin

The thought drifting through my mind,

As I realize what I've committed,

A crime, a sin no one can erase from any record:

I killed the people in that car we hit,

And I've murdered my friends . . .

I didn't take their car keys.

Are You a System?

By Micah Brown

16 years old

Are you a system,
Fostering my care?
Or
Are you a system,
That's just there?
Waiting . . .
For the years to pass,
Till I become an adult . . .
If that's true,
Then your system is really sad.
Why,
When I turn 18,
I have nowhere to go?
I'm just left out here all alone,
No one would ever know,
Who I am,
Or where I'm from . . .
To tell you the truth,
It's been so long . . .
I barely remember my mom.
I have no pictures to remind me!
Just a garbage bag full of clothes . . .
That has always followed me,
From home to home.

Now
I am in the real world,
No family,
Just all alone . . .
Are you a system
Fostering my care?
Or

Are you a system
FosterCARING?
Not really getting a chance of knowing
Who I really am . . .
But only what someone wrote down!
In a file!
On a piece of paper!
Was it their opinion?
Or
Was it what was happening?
Why was my life so bad from the start?
Why didn't I get a chance to utilize my heart?
So that I could feel a mother's love . . .
So that I could experience a special bond . . .
It wasn't fair the way I was born!
Now,
I am out here and this world is cold!

ARE YOU A SYSTEM?

People treat me badly because of where I'm from . . .
What do I say when they ask about me?
Do I tell them the truth?
Or
Do I pretend to be
Something that I'm not?
But just a poor product of a system fostering my care!
YOU NEVER gave me a chance to be a part of a family!
My life wasn't fair.
And you want the world to believe
That you had my BEST interest from the start!
How could that be true?
YOU never knew my heart!
You are just a system!
Pretending that you are listening,
To my wants, my desires, and to my needs . . .
When really,

Your system
Is just all MAKE BELIEVE . . .

The Drain
By Shagari Alleyne
23 years old

This poem is for those who knew someone with an extraordinary gift but due to
       unfit circumstances was not able to fulfill those gifts; thus, his/her life
       was flushed down the drain.
I went down the drain and found the FUTURE of a Could-a-been
(Could-a-been?) someone who wasn't that good but they should've been
Should have been a rapper . . . Lexus coupein'
Should have been a doctor . . . Should have been hoopin'
I grabbed it like "Hell yeah!! This could be mine!!"
BUT . . . history repeats itself without pressing rewind
There's a reason why IT's here
The question is . . . how come?
The beginning might be different but it's always the same outcome
Out comes Martin . . . Out comes Malcolm
It's modern-day slavery. I'm weak I need Balco
Get on your knee (NY) and pay homage to the one who got shot on it
Between the eyes . . . SURPRISE!! . . . no life on it
What convinced him to spray?
This Ass had Sass committed Sin and Ate a life away
Martin wasn't a King. He was more like a Prophet.
My money is in the bank . . . Get your hand out my pocket!!
cuz you can end up wit a commissary
or X'd out of equation BY ANY MEANS NECESSARY
Back to the drain
People going down in vain
High on something other than life . . . Cobain
You can be a rock star like Kurt
But live like him and you will end up in the dirt
The drain

137

The Strength of the Plus Size Woman
By Nikeya Greene

What is the strength of the plus size woman? The plus size woman doesn't need
Howard Stern and his infinite wisdom, to let her know that she is over-
weight . . . thank you very much!
She is greeted by that daunting reality each morning as she showers and dresses
herself . . .
And yet she is still able to simultaneously tell society AND her mirror "So what!
I'm a little fluffy—
Anything THEY can do, I can do better!"
The plus size woman is undeniably female.
She's a mother, sister, aunt, grandmother, teacher, queen of ALL media, model
(yes, I said model!), Academy Award nominee, AND Academy Award
winner, now isn't that precious?
She's beautiful . . . stylish . . . fearless.
And as the debates about her role in society continue to flood the airwaves, she is
DOIN HER THING! Go'n head, beauty queen!
The plus size woman doesn't need YOUR permission to shine!
She will NOT hide her light under a bushel just to pacify your insecurities.
Like it or not, the plus size woman is NOT the minority, she is the MAJORITY!
She is strong, and she's here to stay.

Fashion Fantasy
By Autum Asante
12 years old

Fashion doesn't just sell clothes
It sells dreams
It turns housewives into femme fatales
Teenagers into women
Runway dreams turn into industry nightmares
Rags to riches to rehab

Now Victoria has a secret

138

And you're the last to know
Naked women with white wings
Should have been your first clue
Wearing clothes that don't cover your nakedness
American vogue selling European dreams
Rags to riches to rehab
Suicide and destroyed emotions
Being told you're fabulous
Mrs. J has a prostate, as if you didn't know
A product of an illusion called fashion

Bling bling and being sold dreams
A successful form of self-deception
Girlistic magazines do nothing for low self-esteem
You're the princess of the world
And you're still not seen

America's Top Model giving false images to the dead
Emaciated body types show an industry flaw
Stripped down to mere bones
By fashion vampires who feed on desire
Now 15 and it's time to retire

Just to fit in you have to conform
Not knowing what you're doing
But you need the attention
Poked, touched and insulted

Sex, drugs and depression
Rags to riches to rehab
Anorexia, bulimia and suicide
Death-dealing aesthetics and a ruined self-image
Women drop dead from pressure and madness
So the industry turns a blind eye
Fashion is its own drug
The more you take it

The more you want
Fashion doesn't just sell clothes
It sells dreams
It turns housewives into femme fatales
Teenagers into women
Runway dreams turn into industry nightmares

Girly Teenage Hormones
By Mariam Coker
15 years old

I never really believed
in superstition . . .
but when I saw you
I knew you were different from the others . . .
I was
lucky
to see you cross my
highly hormonal
girly teenage eyes.
You were lovely,
your voice,
your hands,
your eyes,
your smile,
your everything
just got to me.
Then comes the crush stage,
followed by the creeping stage,
followed by "you don't know that I know a lot about you" stage,
followed by the embarassment stage,
and a few rounds of that
leads to
"wow, he would never like me"

the last and saddest stage of
a teenage girl
with hormones pumping into her
just like BP pumped oil
into the Gulf Coast . . .

8.

Haters, Bullies, Someone Who Has Done You Wrong

May a million battered women march out of their graves
and dig their rest in your trembling soul

—Aja Monet

Dave Zirin: What inspired "Haters, Part II," which appears below and on the CD?

Etan Thomas: In "Haters, Part II," I tell the story of reporters who wrote that after my heart surgery, I would never play basketball again. I used this poem as motivation. I would read them or listen to them and be reminded that there were people who expected and sometimes hoped for me to fail.

Dave Zirin: Can you talk a little about how you use writing as a way to combat the negative forces in your life?

Etan Thomas: It's been a positive way of getting out frustration or getting something off my chest. It became a release. When I would have someone who did me wrong or some type of a difficult situation I was dealing with, I would write about it. On the CD you will hear a poem about my first publisher, Jessica Care Moore, who turned out to be the exact opposite of who I thought she was. I had to actually take legal action when she didn't want to pay royalties for *More Than an Athlete*. But everything happens for a reason. People learn from their mistakes and with this situation I definitely learned from mine. My mother's words echo in my mind, "Unfortunately, Etan, not everyone who looks like you is your brother. I know you want it to be that way, but that's not reality." I had to learn that lesson the hard way.

Dave Zirin: This poem on the CD which you call "Medusa" is so intense. It sounds like you were really hurt by this experience

Etan Thomas: Well, Dave, for me it's always worse when Black people treat you like that. It's like if you get pulled over by the police, and you see that he's Black and you give a sigh of relief as if "OK, I'm not going to be harassed or treated unfairly," then he snatches you out of the car, throws you on the hood and yells, "There was a robbery and the punk looks just like you!" It hurts more when that treatment is from someone who looks like you because it is not expected. But I am with a reputable company now in Haymarket Books, and they are carrying *More Than an Athlete*, which will always be special to me because that was my first book. Now I can look back at that whole situation as a learning experience, but yeah, on the CD I had to get a little bit off my chest.

Dave Zirin: What advice do you have for young people who need to get out their frustrations?

Etan Thomas: Poetry can be therapeutic.

Haters, Part II
By Etan Thomas

They said that they doubted if I'd ever play again
Linked me to worst case scenarios and different afflictions
They said that my heart condition would always inhibit the possibility of returning
       to my first love
The life I've been blessed with
They wanted to slash the direction I've been crafting
And stash my dreams in the corners of their side pockets
Erosions of my passions
They wanted to transform the reality of my comeback trail into imaginary notions
Ripple my mind's waves like the movements of oceans
Creep into the crevice of my strength
And hammer it shut with the nail of failure

Reporters
Making their stories colorful like crayons that lay on a book
Leaving the reader to look between the lines of pictures irresponsibly painted
As if what they say is the gospel
They are not hopping out of priestly robes no matter how much the power of the
       pen ascends upon them

They're simply blending truth with fiction
For the sole purpose of winning over the reader's attention
Newspapers force reporters to do the dirty work for the system as they Con-
        doleezza Rice them
Never mind if what they're writing is the truth or based on factual evidence
As long as quality sales remain prevalent
They get a gold star

Rather than passing judgments they should be asking questions
Gathering facts before lashing out baseless opinions
You would think knowing would be half the battle but GI Joe they're not

They've tried to insert doubt into my reality
Leave me tapping out like I'm Savion Glover
Throwing in the towel because I can't take another hit
Words of discouragement and doubt would flood the pages like broken levees
Constant reminders of odds stacked against me
They tried to enlist me in their army of negativity
But I kept ignoring their platters like they were offering pork
See, storks couldn't bring bundles of joy more precious than the power from above
It's over their heads like halos
They couldn't understand that I've found the golden ticket—call me Charlie
And my factory hasn't been condemned
I've got a quicker picker upper stronger than Downy to clean up the filth from
        their pen
It sends strength from within my soul to grant me wishes without rubbing on a lamp
Their words of doubt did not defeat me
I'm standing with two hands in the air like Rudy Huxtable winning a game of
        checkers screaming king me king me

Faith has always been viewed as a waste of time when placed in front of an unen-
        lightened mind
They think that they belong to a cult of divinity
But my sublime serenity
Has entered me from my daily prayers
It holds the remedy to instill in me an inner strength

That is too high for their words to box with
See, they don't understand the power that guides me
When did they become God enough to judge what's inside me

I've sailed past their storm
Sworn never to be discouraged by those who mean me nothing but harm
I'm a child of God
And although lights at the end of tunnels can be difficult to see
And clouded visions can hinder the silver linings that promised to bring up the rear
My faith always told me that a better day was near

Afflictions have been cured
Currents of favor have flowed through me
Blessed me with the ability to endure
His word told me I could
I'm thankful beyond compare
And all I can say is
God is good

Expect More
By Keisha Smith
19 years old

For I am more than your expectations
More than what you make of me
and I'm done trying to be what you expect
done being the me that you made me
and being the me that I am now
I Expect More
For no one has the right to decide me for me
No one has the right to set my limits
I Am More, and you don't know what to make of me
Because you can't hold me down unless I let you
And I'm not letting you anymore because
I Am More

And I care more about what I think than what you think
I believe in my decisions
Even though I am not always right
I see the way you look at me
Like something's wrong because I'm not the way you used to see me
Because I've been held down so long,
and you didn't expect me to be up here with you
Because by doing more than expected, I've caused you to expect more
Well then, Expect More

Stand Up
By Gonna Be Famous
19 years old

The gravel was once so far away,
But it's crashed against my face.
The blood is spilling from my cheek,
Everyone dismissed the thought of my own Grace.

People gather like a herd
Staring at me.
I feel absurd.
Giggles start to build over the school.

Never have I felt so uncool.
The bullies have risen.
But so have I.

I stood and I confessed my fears.
I pulled up courage,
faced my peers . . .

Stand up, be heard.
Leave the nightmares in the past.
Youth like ours will never last . . .

For Once
By Poetic Glow
17 years old

For once
The evening wasn't so dark;
Where usually
I'd spend hours thinking of you

And all the times we've now lost,
That were scattered somewhere along the way;
Down the sea of our sorrows it goes . . .

But yet,
I will not swim to preserve them.
No matter how good the memories may be,
There's just no point in trying if you won't throw me a line . . .

Would you have?
Would you have watched me drown?
Pretending that everything's okay?

Don't answer.
Your silence is enough;
And
It's all you have left.

Well, these words are all that I have left,
And I realize,
For once,
Just how much I don't need you,
Just how much you weren't there . . .

My Eyes

By Jakkie Burten

16 years old

My eyes tell a story that you cannot see
My eyes tell a story about me
Stories of me and where I've been
Stories of me and what I did
Stuff that only I know and try not to show
My eyes are a wall that keeps in the feelings that make me cold
My eyes see what I can see and see what you do not
They see what you see and see what you will not
They see the reasons for why I am the way I am
They see how and why I live the way I live
With my eyes I will survive
With my eyes I will thrive
My eyes are a reason why I am still alive
My eyes see all the lies people put me through
And when I dream all the bad things I want to do to you
My eyes feel the tears trickle down my cheek when I try to sleep
They see when I am weak
My eyes are right
My eyes tell a story of my life

Dedria

By Anonymous

19 years old

No matter how much you claim to have changed you still have to pay the price for
    the things you've done and your price is that you no longer exist
You're a dinosaur
You are no longer welcome in my presence and I would wish you nothing but mis-
    fortune if it wasn't for my little cousin
I would summon child protective services to deem you unfit
Take away your prized possession where it would hurt you the most to hit

I would spit at your pleas to call off the hounds because that's what you would
     deserve
You're an evil bi#?@
I was praying that an ounce of humanity would peek around the corner and the
     monster who is you would switch
But you remained the same
And I pray my lil cousin doesn't inherit your heart's stain
Isn't hampered in life by the repressed animosity of her mother's terrain
It captured your soul and took over your heart
You were filled with envy way greener than pistachio
Mercy, compassion and forgiveness are characteristics that I lack but I can be rational
You're forever isolated on an island all by yourself
When my cousin is old enough to understand I will be glad to explain
That although she has a hateful b@+# for a mother
My love for my little cousin will always remain the same

Bullies
By Beverly Ziegler
16 years old

They're cold, they're cruel, they're clever
What they say stabs like a dagger
Their words punch your insides
Your heart, your mind, your soul
They hurt you on the outside
Like something you can't control

Bullies are a part of everyone's life
This I am sad to say
Bullying is contagious
It darkens everyone's day

It begins when you are small
She pushes you down and you fall
They all laugh in your face

It's a feeling you can't help but hate

They say lighten up
It's just a joke
But bullying is definitely
More than a poke

At first, you desire to obtain what they have—
POWER
You want it. You crave it
You can't live without satisfying this thirst

Then you realize that with this power comes pain
Not your pain but the pain of peers
So you feel regret
You feel remorse

What you thought you'd feel
The Reign, the radiance, the revenge
Isn't worth the sorrow, the sadness, the shame
You know that you need to change

Sometimes it takes someone else
A pal, a parent, a peer
To really see the problem
Someone to interfere

A bully is a vulture
It preys on the weak
So don't be a mouse
The one it easily defeats

Be true to yourself
Stand tall
Turn your back on the bully
Peace is the call

Salem Song

By Brandy Stoner

23 years old

Poor twit
so unaware of it
thinks her son
was named from a movie
but you did it to bruise me
just another way you abuse me.

The name originates
with the tales of King Arthur.
Me and her mate
we loved valor and ardor.
Ironic.
Your commitment was lost
between the pale legs
of a loose boss.

And choice two is that of a queen.
Wasn't aware you still were so mean.
Enough to take the names
of my children.
My womb seems bare
so you steal them.
The babies I dreamed up
can never be real then.

And another thing that's just psycho
is the location
of your engagement photo.
Did you tell her why
it's your favorite?
That the edge of the pond

you're sitting on
was the place where
you pledged before everyone else
God and your dearest
"in sickness and health."

You're a liar.
And I don't entirely buy her
ignorant act. She's a schemer.
Thinks somehow it will redeem her
to make me out
as a terrible partner and parent.
It's transparent. She's insecure
and you're just the one
to twist her.

But she's not innocent.
She's hell-bent.
She lies
and she twists stuff
delights in messing up Christmas
when my daughter's main wish was
to spend the day in my presence.

My baby
has her priorities set
and that's to my credit
because you didn't notice the girl
I was raising.
Until you couldn't hurt me.
Until your words didn't faze me.
It was the only way
to make me pay
for moving on with my life.
I no longer define myself
as that bastard's ex-wife.

Your wedded said
"I usually get what I want."
She can haunt the corners
watching a marriage gasping
drawn to the rasping
but now the vulture is grasping
for my progeny
to marginalize me
so she has more power.

Her feeble mind
gathered some nerve
when you both did something
so absurd and to self-serve.
I can't explain here.
The whole situation
the separation
this anguish I feel.
It's not entirely real
if I don't put it on paper.
She was just another number
in your wallet.
So I called it.
Asked the nature of your relationship.
She describes that as harassment?
I should have kicked her ass then
before she got fat.
The first question she asked
her sibling
was a little thing.
"Is she smaller?"
Not concerned
whether I was taller
or smarter
or kinder

or sweeter.
No explanation
why it took more than three years
to meet her.

You gave her
keeping a job
the names for our babies.
I got fists through the wall
years of your hating.
No hesitation
to throw me into the fire
tell me you did it all
'cause I fail to inspire.

Admitted how much you love
to be cruel
to me.
You broke the rules of humanity.
The promises that you handed me.
So let's just be candid.
We cannot be civil.
Every bit that I give will
be twisted.
Taken a mile.
In a while
I'll change the number
so you can't dial my buttons.

Except for speed dial three.
You knew my baby bear
is more precious to me.
From the moment I felt her
I knew that I'd save her
from abuse
from boys

from the father I gave her.
Remember when
you stood up to tell us
that my love for our child
was making you jealous?

I do. I remember a lot of things.
Finding change for diapers
pawning my diamond rings
getting notices of evictions
losing money for groceries
on your gaming addiction.

I remember leaving my house
leaving you in it.
I remember the truth.
I don't care how you spin it.
Remember your face when I said
"Take it all. I don't need them."
I walked out the door
shrugging
"What price freedom."

It's sick
the ways you show
you're not over me.
The trick is
I wasn't bought or sold.
I'm free.
Hate is still an obsession.
You will be the one
who learns a hard lesson.
Today
you may burn me in effigy
but I can't stay
the common enemy.

The two of you will turn
on each other.

We will stand by and watch it
as daughter and mother.

A Letter to the Statistics
By Sarah Hilware
17 years old

All around this city I see
Subliminal messages that categorize me,
As an at-risk youth for pregnancy, addiction, STDs, depression, suicide . . .
       and the list goes on,
As if the world just checks my gender, race, and socioeconomic status
       and gives up automatically,
As if I am just a label: Black. Pretty-faced. Sex-object. Young. Female.
As if the world just wrote my fable: Smack! There goes another one . . .
My ending is all the same just like the rest,
They all assume that I am mentally incapable of passing life's test,
And they all judge and blame,
Treat me like an experiment . . . If I make it through,
It's against all odds.
They speak to me as if I have never read a book,
Like I never took
That advanced English course,
But every day I force myself to stand tall, walk high, and keep my hopes, dreams,
       and aspirations to the sky,

Because one day, I won't need your penny-enny minimum wage checks!
One day I won't need your Metro!!
And Daddy, as badly as I may want it now, I don't need your child support,
And I'll never ask you to pay it,
Because one day, I won't need your obligated affirmative action financial aid.

I may have to be in debt for a while,
But my success will overshadow all obstacles that I've had to hurdle.

So I say to every statistic and critic that has EVER attempted to crush my spirit
      down to the ground,
Every so-called friend that I trusted wouldn't judge me, but did so in the same mo-
      ments that I was building up that blissful trust,
Every television, radio, magazine ad that was aiming their product at everyone who
      had money . . .
      everyone but me,
Every number, chart, graph, percentage that has tried to define my future,
Every store clerk in Saks 5th Avenue that has looked at me strangely just for being
      in the store,

. . . Thank you all!
I owe you one!
Because the less you believed in me,
The more I believed in myself.

Sing to Me
By Timothy Duwhite
19 years old

She said she promised to always love me
Like Sunday morning mass
On those rare days when the pastor decides not to preach
But "let the choir sing"
Like hymnals sung through braille fingertips
Told me she would be the only woman that could love me blindly
Despite my shortcomings
And I believed her

At birth, I left my paw print in the form of a scar
On the bottom left portion of her belly

I've always been the territorial type
A characteristic she hates about me
For the way it reminded her of my father

"No weapon formed against you shall prosper dear son"
She mutters to me under her breath like insults
Her voice, less back-boned
And more knee-capped
Than I am accustomed to
"Oh what a vile woman you have become"

We used to joke and say
That God created people like us on the 8th day
That split second between 11:59 and Monday morning
Those rare disciples that couldn't be traced back biblically
You always said, "God entrusted us to write our own verses."

But mom, when you claw love poems into the backs of men
Who bare bones to bastard to possibly stay with you
You wield the risk of your words
Running out like people do

And sometimes I wish that instead of human
God molded me into a shot glass
Easier for you to hold
More reason for you to kiss
I would settle on just loving you like bar tabs
You can repay my efforts later

Tell me, did you get any of the letters I've sent you
I stashed a cigarette in the bottom of one of the envelopes
You always said how smoking made you feel closer to God
Reason why you snuck out every time we went to church

Are they treating you well there
Do they really have those rooms where you can scream

Like they promised you
Does it feel anything like a sanctuary

Cause mommy
I was promised direct connection to my father
Within the creases of my palms
Heaven is just a phone call away
Don't listen to what they tell you
You can come back if you want to
AA is supposed to be voluntary

I'm tired of leaving voicemails on tombstones
Be a woman, pick up the receiver
Remind me of why I love you
Or why poems don't seem to mend wounds like they used to

And I wonder
Did the bottom of that bottle taste anything like the heaven you are swallowing now
Did it go down slow, could you hear the gospel within each gulp

I've been sitting here
Trying to decode some sense from these scriptures you left me
About how you could possibly be in a better place
When all I seem to read is that death by self-infliction
Only promises you a ticket to hell
So should the prayers I dedicate to you be in reverse now

"Our Father who art in heaven, hallowed be thy name. Thy kingdom come. Thy
        will be done."
In reverse now:
"Done be will thy. Come kingdom thy. Name thy be hallowed, heaven in art who
        Father our."

Mother
I heard an angel falls from heaven
Each time a sinner catches the spirit

So when the time comes that you need to find me
I'll just be sitting here,
Waiting for the choir to sing

Letter to My Girl
By Tommy Miguel
19 years old

Girl you the best, you the best i ever had . . .
i just can't pinpoint when it all went bad . . .

i'm left ironing out all the wrinkles . . .
caused by your past . . .

got me singing tonight I'm single . . .
sick of you putting my concerns last . . .

you're never wrong and very unapolegetic . . .
not a big deal when you disrespect . . .
all the pain you cause you brush off as if it had no effect . . .
human being with feelings you forget . . .

your dysfunctional definition of what a man is or is not behind your manipulated
        suggested summed up opinion in any situation or problem we have
        comes up to you never being at fault

and through your text message, Twitter, MySpace, Facebook, hypocritical convos
        with your phonies . . .
I'm sweatin you again about being your best friend and now jokes about me being
        a victim yet they are your homies . . .

yet some of them want me
what if I'm feeling lonely?

and you choose like Harold Melvin and the blues having me confused from dissing

my roses and not liking flowers a bit . . .
to saying I don't pay attention to the deeper meaning of it
calla lilies is what I should get
Girl you really need to quit

I can't read your ever changing mind or the future
forgive me for not being man enough to take the blame for all of your issues . . .
lies violence cheating wasn't anything I was used to . . .
so please allow me to excuse you
and accept the apology you never gave me

Miss seeing you son my daddy says my mother got me thinking I'm invincible
and he's absolutely right like the great Mike I'm a smooth criminal . . .
so don't fix your dentals . . . when it's all said and done to apologize about the past . . .

It's that time of the month
I'm just going through some things
Excuses that will no longer last

I Won't Forget
By Damian Andrews
19 years old

I watch movies and dvds to feed my anger
And torment my innermost thoughts
Rotting at the core of my mind is an obsession that keeps me up at night
So I study
Exploring how proper planning can create a lot of creativity
Adebisi and Ryan O'Reily have taught me a lot
Every episode of *Oz* fascinates me
Putting the pieces in their proper place like the movie *Fresh*
The mystery of chest-boxing is like a sword fight
You must think first before you move

Patience is something I'm trying to hold on to with both hands
But I can't seem to relax enough to keep my violent thoughts from being reborn
They keep being warmed back into a big flame
I need to bring this down to a simmer
It's all about timing
Striking at the perfect moment
When the stars are in perfect alignment
And any glimmer of hope to be rescued will be out of his reach
Emotions can't make me stupid
Intelligence has to be at the center of my actions
All sense of inhibition keeps getting lost in my overactive imagination

I'm ready for some get back
Ready to attack my victim and rip his flesh to pieces
Right now I'm anxious
The patience I've tried to hold on to keeps slipping out of my grip
I can only think of justice

I'm sorry I can't take away the hate and love the one who cursed me
The one who wouldn't give me a cup of water when I was thirsty
He wanted it to be all about him
A crab in a barrel that wanted to pull me down to the depths of his level
The height of his limitations
Now I gotta reach him
Past feelings put aside cuz now I gotta teach him

Perpetrating a friend to me
I thought he would die for me
Gliding through lies to me
He can no longer ride with me
See now it's a war and he's not on the side with me

Writing these words I have frightened myself
I am going to try to forgive and put it in God's hands
I can try to be a better man
But it won't be easy

The Body Remembers
By Aja Monet

22 years old

I live in an apartment made of bricks
with a bathroom that sings of a fleeting heart
My kitchen faucet has a sore throat,
ends up in conversations with the skin of my eardrums
At night, I love in silence
dreams of a voice for making love
on white linen, stained with well-worn human
In Octobers, I imagine windows like the ones
along my new lover's spine
Tired of shoveling dirt over the graveyards
on her mother's wrists, a daughter remembers
the switchblades tripping off the ledge of her mother's
tongue, chicken-scratches her insecurities
on the mirrors of her eyelids,
licks suicide off the plate clean like a bulimic torn
between the God that promises heaven
and her stomach, women are tired
of being hungry,
of gritty knees and calloused palms,
tear-stained cheeks and retired songs,
she hums prayers between the fingers of clenched fists
amidst whirlwinds, I wish I could tell this story like a lucid dream,
could stitch heartache like loose strings at the seam
but I am tired of spiraling,
boiling blood
Love doesn't like to be taken advantage of,
lest I need to remind you of the missing artery
in your ribcage
Boy, God ain't make no mistake
when putting a woman into your life
This is for every

man that has ever laid a hand on a woman—
May the wind blow against your skin and you will
feel me, may she smack you the way
I never could
You will die an old man with your hand balled in a fist
at the bottom of the Atlantic, there will be a war
on the terror
May a thousand nails chase you in your sleep,
claw at your flesh like unicorn horns
Angels will tear their wings from their backs
and beat the evil out of you
with them, feathers splattered wet like abstract art
For they will fall in your vanity, wishing to be human
just so they can show you how it is done
May a million battered women march out of their graves
and dig their rest in your trembling soul
and she wishes, she wishes she could say all of these things
but us women are said to have carried our hearts
on our sleeves, always washing laundry
in case it bleeds through the seams

The Green Mile
By Tamara Sease
26 years old

Because of you, I lie here imprisoned.
Trapped within these walls and caught behind these bars in constant remem-
    brance of you.
Oh, how I despise you.
I've never understood how someone so idealistic as you
Could impersonate someone so sincere and authentic as a false precept of truth.
That and those which are real know you as being the reason Jesus exhaled His
    final breath.
His motive for illustrating an expression that only He could demonstrate.
And then here you come.
An image, I'll admit, that took my breath away.

Leaving me an enchanted and captivated young girl
Sprung without cause, yet smiling without care
I was yours, a victim in your pull
Now I just wish you would pull away.

Because of you, I'm serving this sinister sentence because you won't.
As I pace in this frigid cell, I'm reminded of how you misrepresented yourself.
Your comfort was fake and your caress was fleeting.
You made me feel as if I were the chosen one to have met you
But you've impregnated pain within this virgin womb that refuses to miscarry.
Because of you, I sit here, hoping my identity will be called so that I might feel the
    liberty from the grasp of your hands.
The clasp will be broken.
Through these veins, hope will cease its reason, despair will detain its poison, and
    the sentiments of emotion will end.
I will laugh again and dance through evergreens and fields that harvest sanity.
I've emitted so much and gained so little.
I pity the next who crosses your path.
But if her destitution can be prevented through my execution, I'll take the fall.
Guard, I'm ready.
I don't need the cuffs and chains . . . I'll willingly walk the mile.
Finally, Love, you won't live here anymore.

9.
Religion/Spirituality

In the dead of night,
I call your name
to hear no answer.
So long the flame

That once burned so bright
Inside this heart.

Now nothing burns
As I fall apart.
—Vincent Cuccolo

Dave Zirin: What kind of religious upbringing did you have?

Etan Thomas: I was raised in a Christian household. However, I wasn't raised not to think; my mother encouraged thinking. I was the type of kid who had a lot of questions. I remember having long conversations with my childhood pastor Reverend Potter, my mother, and my grandparents about questions I had regarding religion. I studied different religions mostly out of curiosity for what other people believed—from Islam to Judaism, to Mormonism, Catholicism, Rastafarianism, 5 Percenters, Buddhism, and ancient Egyptian religions. I gained a respect for all religions even if I didn't necessarily believe in them. I also learned how men twist religion for their own selfish desires, but that's a whole other topic.

Dave Zirin: Do you consider yourself a religious person today?

Etan Thomas: I consider myself a spiritual person. A personal relationship with God is something that has always been and always will be vital in my life. It's where I gain strength. I am fully aware that I am blessed and none of this would have been possible if not by the grace of God. So I know who to give all praise to.

Dave Zirin: What inspired you to write the poem "Through with Religion"?

Etan Thomas: I was having a conversation with this group of people after a poetry spot one evening. There were a couple of poems read that evening that touched on practices of "the church"—Catholic church scandals, crooked pastors. So religion was the topic of conversation. One girl in particular was very expressive and passionate about her confusion with religion as a whole. She had questions that nobody would or maybe could answer, and this led to her frustration. It was a pretty deep discussion.

Dave Zirin: A lot of young people have questions about religion and question their religious convictions altogether. Based on "Through with Religion," you seem to think this is a healthy, worthwhile process. Can you elaborate on that?

Etan Thomas: I personally don't feel that questioning or wanting to gain a better understanding of what you are being taught to believe in is a bad thing. I was someone who had a million questions growing up, so I asked. Even now, if there is something that I don't understand, I will call or text my pastor—Pastor John Jenkins of First Baptist Church—and ask. How are you ever going to gain clarity if you don't ask?

Through with Religion
By Etan Thomas

She said she was through with it all
She had grown tired of hearing the casting calls to rhetoric
Thought what if it was all one big lie
An attempt to simply comfort our tears and cries
Everything happens for a reason
His ways are not ours
So no matter what the season
Continue to rejoice
Even in sorrow
So even if your prayers are not answered by tomorrow
He's always on time

What if it was just something to make us feel better while life slaps us in the face
        with an opened hand?
Or strikes us with a closed fist

Then stomps us to the ground as we beg for mercy
A ruptured cyst of hate complicated her outlook
Operations couldn't remove the pain from within
Her rose colored glasses were broken
She would begin to see life through lenses of doubt
Questioning existence and infinite possibilities
She shouted for numerous explanations to unanswered questions

She had been angry for many moons
And her pursuit to happiness hit bumps in the road that would darken her sky
As it wrung her mind
Choking the life out of her faith

Why do bad things happen to good people if He cares for us so?

She equated it to Greek mythology
Praying to Poseidon for safe travels across the sea
Or fearing the lightening bolts of Zeus
On an Odysseus type journey across the pitfalls of life
Boobytrapped paths that scattered ashes across the future into plights of gloom

Attempts to make sense of the senseless
Have insight to our vision of things that weren't meant for us to see
An ever existing need of comfortability
Something to hold on to
Grasp within the clasp of our fingers so we can attach the myths to our soul
Wrap our minds around the impossible

Abandoning all forms of intelligence
While He sits up there playing us like a game of chess
Ignoring our helpless calls
Giving us impossible tasks to teach us lessons
While messing with our intellect
Omnipotence makes fools of us all
Listen but don't look
As He cooks our minds with biblical rhymes of infinite interpretations

An abundance of denominations to confuse our minds
We seek to find answers by listening to men of priestly robes
With supposed connections to the divine

Look but don't touch
Just to please His amusement
Tease us with things off limits to our pleasure
Pleasing to the eye
He makes us believe His undying love should guide us away from all forbidden
      fruit

Touch but don't taste
As we're running in a maze
Going in more directions than we can possibly dream of
Interpreting miracles as blessings
That we don't even know to be definitely true

Taste but don't swallow
As hollowed dreams of the afterlife bribe you into doing right
Means of control
Pie in the sky
Threats of hellfire and damnation
Tunes our minds to stations of fright
Ruling with an iron fist
My way or the highway
Enlisting brainwashed soldiers
Patiently awaiting the tribulation
The day of the rapture
Just to capture our compliance
God Fearer
As the end of times is ever growing nearer
We're sent steering through biblical storms
Confused as we can be

People of Faith: A New Kind of Intolerance

By Hyperbole

18 years old

Standing on a street corner holding a campaign sign, I suddenly know.
Know this day could end right here
          right now
     there are people who hate us that much.
Know that things will never be the same
          all the world will know us now.
Know that as much as they chant their chants for equality, they will take it from us
Know that as much as they petition for the right to disagree, they deny us it

Suddenly I know it.
Standing on a street corner holding a campaign sign, suddenly I know.
Know that we will protect what we love
          and what we believe
     no matter what the cost.
Know that we will turn our cheek even though it hurts to be called
          bigots and haters.
Know we will love them because they are our siblings, even when they hate us
Know we are lovers not fighters but we will fight
     "In memory of our God, our religion, and freedom, and our peace, our
     wives and our children."

I know it suddenly.

Note: The quote is from Alma, 46:12 in the Book of Mormon.

Let's Talk about It

By Olajide A. Omojarabi

24 years old

War is the greatest plague that can afflict humanity, it destroys religion, it destroys state,
it destroys families. Any scourge is preferable to it.
—Martin Luther King Jr.

Before writing this article, I inquired from a couple of friends if it would be appropriate to write about the incessant religious crises in Nigeria. Although one of them gave me an emphatic "yes" with suggestions on both local and domestic levels, the other held back his response. "Be careful what you write," his advice was. "You know how delicate the issue of religion is in Nigeria." So when I was editing my draft, I thought of what to include and exclude, and after much contemplation, I took sides with the lady who gave me an affirmative answer. For how long, I thought, are we going to hold back our words on a problem that knows no boundary?

Religious problems are so enormous that every part of the world is affected either overtly or covertly. Take for instance, a northern community where I reside in Nigeria; you can only debate your religious case in private, but can't disclose your concluded action in public. And yet thousands of lives and properties have been lost due to religious crises. In some other parts of the world, the slightest aggression in regard to religion is often met with angry retribution to the point that it has become a topic to avoid in social gatherings. Unfortunately, it is this same issue of religion that has divided some families against each other, and I can say, without any irony whatsoever, that every day lives are lost around the world to one religious problem or another. Why then are we still silent about an issue that, despite its emphasis on faith and spirituality, is gradually giving way to bigotry?

A few days ago, a religious sect in northern Nigeria rose up against Western education, causing all Western institutions in the north to close. According to their belief, Western education is forbidden and so should be completely eradicated from the country. My basic concern is for the few intellects among them who have been brainwashed against education—which promotes knowledge and can help them have fuller, more rewarding lives. This shows the level at which religion can be manipulated by some leaders who, for their own individual aims, poison the minds of people who could have contributed largely to the success and growth of the society and perhaps the world at large. According to Gordon Allport, religion is the audacious bid that binds (human beings) to creation and to the creator. Why then, I wonder, should religious leaders use an act that is based on personal freedom to easily manipulate their people? Why has religion provoked wars and also impelled peace?

In the words of Martin Luther King Jr., "Whatever affects one directly affects all indirectly." Religion is a language that is generally understood around the world, however it is spoken. This means we can avert more problems and forestall more danger. It is not enough to sit in your comfort zone and say, "Religion isn't hurting me personally, so what's the fuss about?" It's about those children out there who have lost either or two parents to religious crisis and those families that have lost their loved ones to peacekeeping in ethno-religious war zones. It's also about the societies that are losing their future leaders to religious bigotry and fanaticism.

Contributing positively to the world is about not only bringing up the best ideas but also combating its societal ills. Think about those small communities you will be saving by just speaking or writing a positive word or two. Speak out and save a soul somewhere. You might heal the world someday. It's a privilege that I have begun the process.

Truth and Religion: Betting on Truth
By Keisha Smith
19 years old

If they proved [the existence of God], they would not keep their words, it is in lacking proofs, that they are not lacking in sense.
—Blaise Pascal

A lot of things in this life exist in shades of gray. You cannot neatly categorize everything into black or white, right or wrong. There are always circumstances, opinions, or other factors that can change the way the world looks at an issue. Take killing, for instance. Our government punishes us for committing murder while organizing gun-carrying armies to take the lives of people. Whether or not this is good or bad is seen as a shade of gray, with arguments both ways.

There are no shades of gray when dealing with the truth. For argument's sake, if the truth happened to be that killing is wrong in all circumstances, then government-funded organized killing is wrong, the death penalty is wrong, etc. It wouldn't mean that there will be no killing; it would just means that it is a fact that killing is wrong. The problem with truth is that a lot of times we do not know what is true, but that does not mean that the truth does not exist.

When it comes to the existence of God, there are two possible truths. Either God does exist, or He doesn't. Many people say that we as humans have no way of knowing 100% if God does or does not exist. Pascal's argument challenges humans to look at religion as a bet, and see if it can develop into something more over time. He believes the possible payoff of being religious is eternal happiness in heaven instead of eternal pain in hell, while the possible payoff of rejecting religion is only good for a few short years on earth.

Pascal says, "The uncertainty of the gain is proportioned to the certainty of the stake, according to the proportions of the chances of gain and loss." Pascal is saying that the smart thing to do, even if you do not believe in God, is to practice a religion just because the possible positives outweigh the possible negatives. I do not believe that this bet is the best way to ensure your spot in heaven. In fact, I find it incredibly silly and superstitious.

This argument is practically comparing God to a game at a casino where you call out a number and hope that's where it lands. In this case there are only two numbers, so you have a 50-50 shot, one being true and one being false. You are betting on truth, hoping to claim your prize, because if you bet on false and it lands on true you are afraid of punishment. But life is not a game, and truth is not something that happens by chance, so Pascal's comparison makes no sense. When you bet on something you hope for it instead of believing in it. In order to believe in something, you must believe it to be true. You must believe it with all your heart and knowledge. You cannot "bluff" religion.

Pascal also talks about people having the will to believe while being skeptical. He says that by going to church and following God's word without believing it to be true, people will actually start to believe because the belief sets of their peers may rub off on them. While I think it can be helpful to some to feel a sense of community in their religion, the fact of the matter is that religion is a personal relationship between one person and God. If the person is only willing to behave righteously, but is not willing to open up to the reason why they are behaving this way, then that's no good. Also, you are lying to the community of people you are seeking salvation from.

You must realize that according to the Bible salvation doesn't come from saying "I believe in God" or from acting godly; it comes from honestly believing in God and, secondly, having God inspire you to act saintly. You will do it because you believe it is right. If someone you meet in the church community does something that inspires you to truly believe, that is great, but if you are seeking salvation from people or actions instead of God, then that defies the point.

During a person's life it is natural for them to wonder about the world and seek the truth. And whether God exists or not is a truth that affects the world and any person's everyday life in many ways. Our belief in God shapes the way we view our world, shapes the way we view ourselves, and shapes the way we view right and wrong. If there is no God, then this world is an accident and everything is random, we humans are not special, and there is no good or bad, just choices and consequences. Then there is no right or wrong, only bets.

Whether or not God is real is a debate that has been going on for a long time, and it is very unlikely that it will be settled anytime soon. I disagree with Pascal's argument. You cannot gamble with a belief, you cannot bluff God, and you cannot "act out" religion. Life is way too important to leave to chance. There is only one truth, so we all must do what we feel in our hearts to be right.

I Have Two Hands
By Virginia Murphy
19 years old

I have two hands
Two simple hands
Hands made of bone, flesh, skin, and peach hair
I have two hands that do work
They will work until my one heart stops beating
They will be worked to bone
They will be tired and restless
I have two strong hands
Hands that hold force when malice gets the better of my one mind
Hands that hold the most fragile of things, things that can break and snap
I have two soft hands
Softened from the finest of soaps and lathers
Softened from tears that dropped in them when my two hands were the only
        things that could wipe them away
Softened for days of work and days of play and days of being clean and days of
        being dirty
I have two hands
Two hands that join in prayer when I need it most
Two hands to guide me in the night when it is too dark to see
Two hands to embrace your body when you need it most
Two hands for him to hold

Two hands that try to hold onto humanity as insanity spills into its veins and poisons its mind

One hand to write the dearest, sweetest of affections to the closest of family

The other hand to hold the page from slipping away

These two hands given to me by the Almighty

These two hands given to me by birth

Almighty blessed these hands to make me strong

My two hands are HIS creations

My two hands were clean when HE sculpted them from the clay

My two hands are now dirty, stained with sins and the Devil's dirt

These two hands, this one body, these two legs and arms, this one mouth, two eyes and ears, and this one mind of mine will soak in the water of Holiness before Almighty HIMSELF says that my time of bathing with these two filthy hands is done

I have two hands

Two simple hands

Stained with sin and the Devil's dirt

Dead hands

like a nightmare from the past

There are ghosts all around me

holding me still

I can't escape their invisible clutches

even though I can see through them

I cannot see past them

I can't move, they're all around

The ghost of the dead breathes all my air

I'm suffocating from standing still

in invisible hands

here so long, it's all I can remember

So that even if I realized the truth:

That dead hands cannot bind me

I cannot escape

I don't remember how to walk

I don't know how to breathe

So I hope I can remember

Before I run out of air

Gray
By Vincent Cuccolo
17 years old

In the dead of night,
I call your name

To hear no answer.
So long the flame

That once burned so bright
Inside this heart.

Now nothing burns
As I fall apart.

Chest now cold,
It's here to stay.

Where are you, God?
My world's gone gray . . .

Black Church
By Kosi Dunn
17 years old

At an Easter vigil in a deaf church
I lit a candle
they told me it's because
a black man let people
beat
cut
stab
hate

him into a tree
told me it's because
he loved us
I ask
"so why do we burn candles?"
. . . realize.
How else does dead flesh change living?
Keep the fire going.

A Moment of Fatherhood
By Concept 87
19 years old

The moment began just as any new father's blessing . . .
Little did I know that it would end in a painfully learned lesson,
That the trying of my faith would be brought on through great grief
In the disguise of a blessing that would be so brief.

I was relieved from graveyard shift at 2:00 in the morn.
Arms cramping up behind the wheel as I dozed off and lightly smacked my head
    on the horn.
I then got a call on my phone with my skin tattered and worn.
My mother's voice said, "Justin, get to Bethesda North! Stacey's in labor, your little
    girl's about to be born."

I made the biggest U-ie in history on I-71.
Doing 90 with tunnel vision as my neck slowly started to lunge,
I finally got to the overpass and my heart came to suddenly plunge
because two people were arguing in the intersection about a car that had been
    shunned.
I muttered, "Ain't this bout a . . . beep! Can we move this along?"
Meanwhile the police officer simply sat and took notes like this was the same sad
    song.
I quickly called my mom on my phone speed dial.

No answer so I left a message saying "Mom, I'm caught in a dumb dumb's car
wreck, I may be a while."

Finally, half an hour later, they directed us through.
Still rushing because the baby was about 20 minutes overdue,
I made it to the front desk and the receptionist and made my way passing a series
of empty rooms, hoping to see the face of the child who just left my wife's
womb.

I found the doctor who handled the procedure, and said, "Are you Doctor Bret?"
He said, "Yes, sir. Who are you?" I said, "Hold up, just let me catch my breath . . ."
I told him who I was and explained what took me so long.
He said, "Sir, I'm very sorry but they're both gone."

I said, "Gone? Oh you mean to recovery. Well, let's go, show me the way."
He said, "No, you're not hearing what I'm trying to say. Your daughter strangled
as your wife pushed as her throat was in the umbilical cord, caught. As a
result your wife's artery ruptured and her heart went into cardiac arrest
until it finally stopped."

All function was cut from my brain, and numbness spread throughout my arms
and my legs.
I dropped to the floor and hit my head so they quickly got me a bed.
I saw the lips of the doctor mumble, but I didn't hear a word that he said
As tears streamed down the crevices of my face and blood dried at the back of my
head.

In three hours I was released and mindlessly drove toward my lonely home.
I then slowly drifted to the shoulder and finally off the edge of the road.
I slowly approached a ravine and before the 200-foot fall
I looked around as I heard a voice by which my name was called.
It said "O, ye of little faith, lower your head and rest
Because you know better than most that this is only a test."
Tears rapidly ran down my face and I didn't know what to say or do . . .
So I simply looked up and tearfully muttered, "God, why, how could you . . .

"You're the one who sent me Stacey so you knew the love that we had.
You've taken not only that, but the prospect of me becoming a dad?"
Overwhelmed, I hopped out of the car and started walking and yelling abroad.
The voice said, "Be still and know that I am God!"

I dropped to my knees and slowly began to drown in my own tears.
Finally, I almost felt the touch of God as He said, "My son, lend me your ears . . .
Your faith has always been strong through its tests and trials,
So why, after what I've brought you through, are you doubting Me now?

"You've known Me to be a God of restoration, giving you more than what you've
        lost . . .
And I know it seems that you're paying too high of a cost.
But you must know, what I am doing is done for your good,
And that I love you more than anything in creation ever would."

All I could do was close my eyes and lower my head,
And when I opened them again I found myself in bed.
My wife was at my side and my unborn child was still in the womb sown.
I simply sat and reflected on everything God had shown.

To you parents going through loss, I can't say I know how you feel,
How you manage to stay sane, or cope daily to deal . . .
But I'm convinced that God sees you out of the corner of His eye
And although you may occasionally gaze deep into the night sky and ask the Lord why,

You have to know that He loves you, and that He has a divinely constructed plan
And often times it's not built in a manner set for us to understand.
But set Him as your hiding place and contemplate on how He has been so good
And do your best to cherish the blessed thoughts from your moments of parenthood.

Laplace's Equation
By Clarissa Moore
22 years old

Laplace's Equation, Sigma, Pi, Rotation, Spheres of Sound are Near, If only my mind were clear. I can see harmony, I can see infinity, Zero, a Function of a fractalated mind trapped in time. A fourth dimension, a fifth, a sixth, Newton saves me from Dissension. And soon my soul will not feel as sick. Atom shaped, Gyrating quakes, A single Key will sound, When this secret it is found, I will be salvation. Science saves me, Precision paves me, Ambition starves my craving. For freer thought, A better view, I won't get caught, Beneath their pew. No sacrifice, but blood and sweat. No edifice, but love atomic. Function Harmonic, feel my body quake, inspired infinitely by I. This is the best high.

Unrestricted
By Tamara Sease
26 years old

I was bound. Stuck and stagnant in a posture of immobility. Tangled, twisted, strangled, and fixated on a circumstance I couldn't solve; so restricted and confined that even the simplicity to breathe was breathtaking. Held by what, you ask? Chains.

Chains of rejected relationships . . . men who embedded in my mind that I was no more than a temporary moment of satisfaction. Chains of insecurity . . . society's very own images implanted in my mind of what I should look like. Chains of fear . . . terrified, petrified, and horrified to trust a soul; frightened to open up and simply express the liberty of being nothing but me.

Chains of expectancy.
Chains of doubt.
Chains of guilt, regret, and anxiety.

I was confused; left frustrated, neglected, rejected, negated, and disclaimed. Bound to a life I wanted to escape, but daylight always seemed so untouchable, so unreachable, so far away.

But one day the wind blew. And one day the sky opened. And one day the sun did appear. From a horizon far off, I was encountered by a love that removed all that festered inside. Under shades of lavender and violet, it held the gentility of a serenity I wanted to know. It was Christ that showed me the error of my ways and lifted the heaviness of those chains that held me so inhibited and repressed to the point where removing them relieved the weight of the world.

Finally, I can see who I am in Him.

Finally I'm recognizing the light He placed in me.

Finally, breathing and smiling and laughing the way my destiny designed me to be. Finally, I'm unrestricted to just . . . live.

What Spirituality Means to Me
By C. J. Lowe
19 years old

My first recollection of religion includes good night prayers and morning feel goods. While spending the night at my father's parents' house, Grandmother, as we affectionately called her, would pray with us before bed. Grandmother would teach us the Lord's Prayer and tuck us in. In the morning Grandmother made sure that we woke up giving thanks to God for waking us up and asking for his protection throughout the day. In the morning Grandpa would always cook breakfast. We were awakened by the smell of bacon and the strumming of a guitar. Grandpa loved to cook and croon. As the years went on they would impart more and more in our lives. One thing you knew about spending Saturday nights at Grandmother's is that Sunday morning you were definitely going to church. Grandmother attended a C.O.G.I.C. (Church of God in Christ) church. Basically she was Pentecostal. Grandmother's church usually lasted about 3 to 4 hours. You were guaranteed to see some whooping, hollering, tongue speaking, spirit fainting, aisle sprinting, choir singing, glory giving, testifying church. And my grandmother was at church anytime the doors were open. In fact, to this day, even in her failing health, Grandmother (who can't make it to church) has her television tuned in to the gospel channel. My grandparents have been married for over 60 years. I don't know if my grandmother wore my grandpa out with her churchgoing, but as long as I can remember I've only seen my grandpa in church for weddings and/or funerals. I'm not saying that Grandpa was not spiritual. He would always bless the food, read us Bible stories, and talk about how far God has brought him. His favorite Bible verse is Philippians 4:13, "I can do all things through Christ which strengthens me."

Grandpa didn't do a lot of preaching, but he would always instill the importance of family, a good work ethic, and being kind to others. Take Grandmother and Grandpa together and it made for a perfect balance of being good and doing good.

My grandparents were my first recollection, but my parents raised me in the church. My parents were divorced when I was very young. In fact, they were quite young when they had me and not much older when they were divorced. Separately they both went to church and were active in their church homes. My parents, both Christian, were a part of different denominations while I was growing up. My father, whom I visited one weekend a month, attended a Baptist church. My dad was in the choir and instilled the importance of serving. He stated that service brought so many blessings. My dad would always say, "What an awesome God we SERVE." At an early age I watched my father serve in the church. From singing in the choir to directing it, from being in the men's group to teaching Wednesday night service, my dad had a heart of service. To him serving in the church was a major part of going to church. My mother kept me in church while I was growing up. Going to church with my mom is where I received the majority of my spiritual food as a babe in Christ. My mom, who felt it was important to know Christ, helped me to learn who I am in Christ. I was baptized at a young age and learned that Christ was my intercessor, redeemer, and savior. My mother felt that it was her job to keep me rooted in the word. Church was not playtime. Even as a child I was expected to not only hear the word but be a doer of the word. I gave my life to Christ at the age of 9. Going to church with my mom I received lessons in love, faith, forgiveness, and righteousness—all of which are the core to Christianity in my opinion.

My spirituality, with some life experiences sprinkled in, has made me into the person I am today. I have taken many lessons learned from the most significant people in my life to shape and mold not only myself but how I view the world. My grandmother taught me about the power of prayer. Today I take all my problems to the Lord in prayer. From that I learned not to worry about the problem.

Spirituality has played an important part of my life. It has shaped and molded me so much from childhood. It is exactly the reason why I think it should play such an important part of my children's lives. My spirituality has made me into the man, the husband, the father, the son I am today. It is my prayer that the same can be said by my children when they are grown.

10.
Police Brutality

He's been on the force for 17 years and every
time tears are shed and accusations of brutality
and racism and abuse run wild like loose savages
that roam the inner cities he shakes his head
and says it's a pity only one perspective
is ever seen

—Stefan Jacobs

Dave Zirin: From the outset of your poem "Pigs," you make it clear that "there are two types of law enforcers." How has your personal experience shaped this outlook?

Etan Thomas: I have experienced firsthand the ugly, corrupt side of law enforcers. I have been harassed, stopped repeatedly for no reason, searched and treated like a criminal. One of the first speeches I wrote in high school was after a policeman stopped me on my way to a game. He called for backup and detained me for a long time because he thought he had seen my face in a lineup. Turned out he had seen me in the papers because of basketball. They actually had me handcuffed and sitting on the curb, and I was late for one of the biggest games of the year. Unfortunately, that wasn't my last encounter with that side of police.

Dave Zirin: It would appear that most of the young people in this chapter will agree with your assessment and may even take it a step further. As the rapper Drake says, "21 years and I ain't never met a good cop." How do you keep from labeling all police officers?

Etan Thomas: Let me be clear. I do not feel that all police officers are pigs, and I can't make the same statement that Drake made. I do feel that too many choose to be pigs, but it is important to keep in mind that not all police officers are cut from that same ugly cloth. I have personally dealt with many police officers throughout

183

my entire life that I not only look at with respect and honor, but that I am thankful to for serving the community and patrolling the streets. I have worked with police officers who have Scared Straight programs with the goal in mind of helping young people make the right decisions. Simply put, there are good police officers as well as bad police officers, and while I do sincerely believe that the good ones far outweigh the bad, police brutality remains a crucial issue in today's society.

Dave Zirin: What do you think needs to be done to ensure that all officers of the law act justly?

Etan Thomas: I think they have to be held responsible for their actions and receive proper punishments. I can name case after case in which police brutality occurred and initially it was made into a big deal and shown throughout the news. The officers may even have been suspended—with pay—pending an investigation, but as time went by and the story died down, it gets swept under the rug. The officers return to work as if nothing happened, and it's back to business as usual. That's not being held accountable.

Pigs
By Etan Thomas

There are two types of law enforcers
Respectable hardworking honorable police officers who protect and serve, risk
      their lives every day to keep our streets safe and clean
And then there are Pigs

How many times does the image of the police abusing their power have to flood
      the gates of our reality before something is done?

Their rescue from manhood is wrapped around their badge and their gun
They give good policemen a bad name
Entertaining corruption while playing productions of destruction's flute
Orchestrating symphonies of planted evidence senseless beatings and harassment
      just to name a few
Coerced confessions falsified police reports and Giuliani allowing corruption
      within New York's pigs in blue
He's no choirboy—plungers and 41 shots are the songs they choose
Videotaped beatings entering without a warrant and illegal search and seizure as
      they'll hold you without process due

They've blown their evil through the windpipes of time
Conducting crimes of endless lines to blacken the skies of their chosen victims
Drunk with power they've showered the multitudes through christened realities
Created normalities for societies that stretched across the land of the free
Chests poked out with feelings of invincibility
From Virginia to Georgia New York to Tulsa L.A. to Texas
Beaming lights of Napoleon complexes
Reflective glasses teaching classes of contempt
Moving targets in the bull's-eye of their scope
They've soaked the masses with sponges of evil
Laying cups of iniquity on malevolent coasters
Bullets of contempt armed with wickedness and hate in their holsters

Vampire eyes
Scrounging through the darkness of the night to wreak havoc on the day
They pounce on their prey with the fangs of a predator
While their captives remain motionless
As if comatose by a sedative
But that doesn't stop their madness
Commanded to freeze
Hands held high or behind their back
Hostage position on bended knees
They're granted the authority to sink their teeth into the necks of their captives
They move in for the kill
Endangering a species like raptors
Throughout the streets a river of blood will fill
Steal kill and destroy
While we're numb to the pain like injected novocain
We've become accustomed to their replayed scenes of horror

Bending frames like plexiglas
Calloused schemes of malice dreams
They've built palaces to execute their tactical themes
When will it end

FTP

By Nyles Thompson

19 years old

American police have killed more citizens with bullets
Than the amount of casualties in all the wars and all terrorist
Attacks since Vietnam.

Since the year 2000 more American civilians have been killed by
Police gunfire than the number of casualties in 9-11.
Few of these state sanctioned murders have ever faced convictions
Or due process in a jury trial.

A one room flat, a hoodie and a baseball bat.
Keep my eye on the door and my mind on the paper to stack.
Flip the channel on the 12-inch screen—
another shooting up in Boston, an undercover d-t.
He, new to the scene, minority teen, they swore it was weed.
Checkin forensics and the whole car is clean.
It only took an hour to acquit the beast,
A imminent danger charge to justify the means.
Flip another channel, I'm horrified to see
South-side Atlanta and the sarge keep clean,
Speakin to the news with intent to deceive.
A 92-year-old woman they sayin she flood streets.
Middle of the night, they moving like white sheets.
Got the no knock warrant, they comin with big heat.
Civil rights march we looking for young leaders.
We goin all scream to re-up till they all free Mumia.

Black Target Practice
By Chelsea Cobb
15 years old

Pavement jungle gyms in Queens let the chimpanzees play Red Rover with the law.

Black men on streets is a dead man walking and a target for cop's bullets.

Cops are fashion consultants.

So in police fashion, red looks good with black

so they rearrange African American wardrobes with bullet caps

lodged in red hearts.

Are you with the trend today?

Sean Bell fell victim to this new craze when 50 shots pierced his heart.

Cops are preachers.

And their guns their bibles and with these 50 holy caps

that penetrate dark skinned organs

will be baptized by Sean Bell's dark skinned blood,

in hopes that they can replenish his soul of the monstrous demons.

Sean Bell's wedding bells rang 50 times and his should have been wife

waits for her should have been husband.

Their relationship divorced when the gun and bullet separated.

It's different when the battered body you step over in the street is your husband.

Cops are garbage truck drivers.

They say black men are breathing garbage

so police brutality isn't the right term.

They're doing you a favor to help clean up these streets.

Can't you see?

Cops are magicians.

They love to watch black men levitate.

Even during slavery, they performed magic tricks for master,

levitating from weighted weeping willows heaving black bodies.

To driving whips across Sunset Boulevard

from thrashing whips across their blood spattered black backs.

To chains hanging from dark rinse jeans

from dark skinned dreams hanging by chains from trees.

To bobbing rhythmic heads to that fly beat

from bobbing dying heads, their soles above five feet.
From busting moves to busting caps, pop locking to popping gats.
When cops shoot, they should aim towards their sole
so they can dance along the injustice like monkeys on stage.
Cops should write Bible scriptures on bullets
so when a black man dies, he'll tell God
that He is in his heart.
Cops should aim at a black man's face so the features are so distorted
detectives would have to rely on the color of their skin.
Because that's why they're shooting, right?
We are forced to believe that they're skin is
too brown to be a man,
too dark to be a father,
too black to be a husband.
As the cop prayer goes,
"By the power invested in me, these bullets shall rid
every drug dealer,
every deadbeat dad,
every murderer,
every gangster,
every rapist.
Every black man on these blood streaked streets."
Let the police say,
"Amen."

Serve and Protect
By Max Turner
19 years old

Serve and protect
More like hurt and neglect
Demand our respect
Any criticisms and they upset
Starting fake programs to befriend us

But when the time come they never there to defend us
Pretenders
My skin gets me searched every time I get stopped
But then you upset when I don't give tips to crime watch
On the news acting like they care for my community
But anytime you get a chance look at what they do to me
Beat us brutally
While they hide behind a badge
Follow drug dealers and take they drugs and they cash
And I'm in a gang just because I wear a chain
Police been beating minorities for years
That's like a police protocol
But MY race
Makes ME a thug
Subdue me with jabs, kicks, and billy clubs
Even use tasers and handguns if the billy clubs don't work well enough
Then it's covered up,
Officers on a paid suspension
Under investigation
Until the case loses attention
A few officers got charged
Can't recall no convictions
But I'm overreacting for being pulled over daily for fitting the description
Ain't saying they all bad
Got to be a few clean ones
And they probably great
It's that I just haven't seen 'em
Police got a checkered past from Los Angeles to New Jersey
It's like they are bred and designed to hurt me
And the difference between the police 40 years ago and today is
Back then they openly recruited police that were racist

Como Police Incident

By Alan Giles

19 years old

This is what they want to hear

Mr. Officer I promise my testosterone at home
I'm terrified of the thought of me sopping from your chrome
Yazza gon' and check, ain't nothin' but a phone
I'ze gon' do what ya tell me ain't nothin' in my dome
"Constitution" whuh? I can't hardly pronounce that!
No sir officer, where you say that you found that?
Not mine sir, no, I would never lie, never to a clever guy such as yourself
It's them uppity blacks who dreaming about touching your wealth,
Them blacks who read, I'm happy I'm not up in a tree!
You god-like Caucasians made this nation
—really, nothin' ta see here I'ze jus' happy ta be here—
Befo' y'all, sir, jus' apes in phases
I hate uppity black folks tryna say its racist
Can we please go back to when we knew our places?
That old feeling back, please use those bracelets

I can't do that coon swag for no po-lice
I hope he don't sniff the true man on me
All them weapons now you brave officer
I still take you back to the cave officer
Why you need six devils to one god
One whole squad killing one brother like y'all hard?
Black like I spent the whole summer in yo' yard
In this evil pit no wonder we go off
—You gotta give 'em that brother who so soft,
You give 'em a real brotha and watch how quickly they thrown off
They get acquitted for killin' brothas I'ma tuck two
Since when did being a human being become treason to you?
The educated placated by dumb reasons?

Now they got me in a cage in fact, for what?
Cuz now it's hunting season?
They want us in they field or underneath it,
I'm in the courthouse, nine panel mural
of American settlement all them white men heroes
Spanning 200 years not a single Negro?
Crook in a black robe, I may not be that old, but
I'm not picking up justice from this judge
And now my story is told

Right or Wrong
By Marco Vann
16 years old

I open the door and see police officers
I see them frowning upon me
To see them, notice them, and hear them
And I see a person with unused anger

Police officers using unnecessary force have been here for years
From slavery, to segregation, to the present of today
It's been used for generations by officers of the law
And it certainly is wrong

They use the simple excuse "resisting arrest"
Planting items on the victim
But really it's just brutality
And it too is wrong

However, some criminals need brutality
Whether the case is murder, rape, or robbery
These people are the downside to people alike
And brutality in this form is right

I see on the streets men hustling and gang banging
Girls on the street popping, locking, and bouncing
And police take them down one by one
And this too is wrong

People see the police and are afraid
They're even scared to where they won't even talk
They see a brutal force that is a liar
And those people are right

Police brutality has its time though
When a man does resist arrest
Or when a person attacks an officer
That is when brutality is right

To me my point is simple
It has a form
and it's everywhere

No matter where you go
The police sure don't know
They're right and they're wrong will always show
But us we'll never know

Police brutality right or wrong
It can go away
From a traffic stop to an escapade
Its brutal way can't be tamed

But people like us can shut it down
By getting involved in the legal way
Who cares if it takes years
Police brutality will take no fear

Misdirected Blame
By Stefan Jacobs
19 years old

If they're going to act like animals they should be treated like animals is what my
    father always says
If they want respect they have to behave in a respectable manner
He's been on the force for 17 years and every time tears are shed and accusations
    of brutality and racism and abuse run wild like loose savages that roam
    the inner cities he shakes his head and says it's a pity only one perspec-
    tive is ever seen
There are two sides to every story
Investigations and suspensions before knowing all of the facts
Relying on taped moments without showing the full occurrence
What happened before and after could change your opinion
It could switch your decision to assign immediate guilt to a party not guilty of any
    crime but upholding the law
When it is not shown how the incident started
Thousands of judgments are thrown in the directions of heroes as zeros are held
    up as victims
It's sickening
We wouldn't be able to survive as a society without law enforcement
Sometimes they have to be enforced in order to fully protect
They risk their neck for the safety of all

The Color Blue Hurts More
Than the Color Purple
By Christian Lewis-Davis
18 years old

We're all enemies of the state
guilty before even testified
we're the us in justice
because it's just us that's getting harassed on the daily

it's the norm
a cop on a kid like a dog on a fire hydrant
they used to be black-ops or black cops specialists
widening their branch like State Farm
we're on your side . . . only in commercials you see
put it on the streets it looks like what is shouldn't be
we the people can't take too much abuse
we the children couldn't be more confused
aren't the bad guys supposed to be targeted
not the people who just learned how to spell what target is
when double digits hit
like comic flicks wow pow
as for batman he's a black man
a vigilante a rule breaker
but never naughty by nature
looking for the benefit in you and I
why may I be who I of completely
pause and let's rewind the time
skin color wasn't hunted for gold
. . . wait no it was
so history's repeated
so some minds still believe wrongs went right
that's a lie it's all left
left as is as a code
written in the stone
signed Willie Lynch among other demonic maleficent creatures
who were intelligent
leap the slaves no, blacks no, coloreds no, so said citizens in line
no break for liberation
no break for humankind
make the new uniform blue
so when stains of first blood get on
you have all colors of blood worn

11.

Guns, Violence, Street Life

This was not the last time your edges would become
ruddy and stain the bank red
with early morning passion
— Taylor Johnson

Dave Zirin: How would you describe the pieces included in this section and your piece as well?

Etan Thomas: The poems I received on this topic were more than troubling; they were tragedies. With all of the senseless killings that have taken the lives of so many young people, this is a topic that cannot be ignored. So many young people have taken to a life of crime fearing that this is the only way for them to achieve their goals in life. Intelligent, gifted, talented young people who could be anything they want to be far too often choose to go down a road where the only two options are dead or in jail. While I do not possess the answer to this problem, I wanted to speak simply as a person who is tired of seeing so many young people go down that path.

Dave Zirin: Were you subjected to street violence growing up in Tulsa?

Etan Thomas: Personally, no. Growing up I had no desire to join a gang or enter into a life of crime. That's just not where my head was. I was focused on playing ball, hanging with my boys, speech and debate, learning about my culture, especially after reading *The Autobiography of Malcolm X*—in middle school. That book opened my eyes to the world around me.

Dave Zirin: Then what is it that has led you to work with young people who have been?

Etan Thomas: I had a lot of friends, guys I played ball with, go down that road. I always make the point clear that I can think back to the people I grew up around between New York and Oklahoma, and I can easily name 30 guys who I know should've made it to the NBA before me, but just made bad decisions and took different paths. I had friends that joined gangs, started selling drugs, stealing, robbing, doing anything to make money. I have had way too many people I know end up in prison or killed, and unfortunately, it doesn't seem as though things are getting better with the younger generation.

Wake Up
by Etan Thomas

Cats be earning bachelor degrees in thuggenometry
Embracing the art of criminal mind-states
Sharper than switchblades
But tattooed in their mind states
Is only how to get paid

Watching replayed outcomes on previously previewed movie reels
Scared to do what's right
Intelligent but spineless they're Michael Steele

Just enough for the city they're focused on living
Possibilities are limited
As futures remain inhibited
Their eyes only on dollar signs

Plunging to their deaths like a hard headed Icarus trying to fly to the heavens

Patterns of illegal endeavors never cease to amaze me
Mental fixations create scenes of horror
Tales of incarceration are glorified as if prison is an entertaining place to be
Problematic endeavors are yelling charge at the top of their lungs
As we're sprung like coils hanging from trees in Mississippi
Hung like chandeliers

Yeah we've been done wrong but we do each other worse
The curse we're protecting

The connection with the plans of our oppressors

Electing officials who inhibit our production
While we increase the appetite for our own destruction
Planting smiles on the faces of politicians who place our heads on the mantel as
their prized conviction
Then brag about being tough on crime to pale faces who feel safer with us behind bars

But your screaming thug life
Leading paths of unrighteous

Drug dealers
Coming through like vampires in the night
Bloodsucking monsters injecting poison in the veins of faces that resemble their own
Treasonous overtones
The author of pain and tears
Creators of cries and moans
Dedicated to our annihilation
Ignoring reflections of familiarity
Mirrored images bring forth no hesitation
Planting seeds of death
Criminality's emergence
Evil horses stampeding through the forest of greed
Swollen bellies fail to serve as deterrents
A robbery of innocence

Dollar signs have corrupted minds as well as souls
Stolen possibilities
Levitating darkened clouds to enhance instability
Engulfed in self hate
You've banged your gavel sentencing the multitudes to a lifetime of addiction
Lacerating lifelines with damaged mental states
Without the possibility of parole
Have you ever seen a newborn crack baby
With the piercing sound of addiction's call?
Have you heard the uncontrollable screams that seem to echo off of every wall?

A scene of horror
Because that baby is now going through a state of withdrawal
Dependent at an early age
Body shaking as she craves a poison at a few hours old
The coldest of winter's discontent
The consequence of a drug dealer's allegiance
That over the course of time will prove to be a crime of extremity

As time marches on she doesn't learn to crawl or walk on schedule because she's
        got deformities
Everything's a step or five behind so an abnormal life proves to be inevitable
Physically and mentally she becomes socially blind
Dyslexia
Brain damage
God only knows what else

Maybe she can go to school but it's difficult for her to learn
Even if she yearns to readjust the imbalance of her mind's inherited flaw
She remains trapped in the damage that comes from within
And she's violent so she gets in trouble with the law

Unable to form any kind of close ties
So she's faced with the prospect of going through her miserable life alone
Her possibilities have been hereditarily torn
And they are being born by the truckloads
Millions of an entire generation of our people who are being destroyed before they
        are even born
They are still creating mind states to fill the new prisons they build
The thieves in the night are still lurking
With us still focused in the middle of their scope like public enemy
Why do we keep walking toward the target
Disregarding the way of the light?
Avoiding warning signs allowing them to bind our minds at the heels
We wallow in the slop they poured to devour our souls
Stunt our mental growth
Deflate our passions to rationed possibilities

Sports music entertainment or a life of crime as our destiny
Don't let them limit your future
Victims of circumstance can't murder your fire
Your film of potential can't remain undeveloped
Stop listening to the lessons of willie lynch

A wise man once said
I'm tired of watching my brothas waste their lives
And letting warner brothers depict them
Our soldiers are strong but it's been too long pumping fist and frying chicken

We're better than that
Descendants of kings
As Marcus Garvey would say
Up my mighty race
And realize how special you can be

Breathe into Me
By Mackiel Benson
14 years old

Stricken, fallen, flung down upon the ground
Afraid, trembling, with no one but my shadow to hold
It's too late now, it's too late now
I've been erased, without a sound
You said not to cry, you said it was all right
just a scratch, nothing more, just a bruise
it wasn't anything you said, it didn't hurt
it wasn't even really worth calling it a fight
I was scared to answer the door
You knew that, right? You were so mad
If only I'd had dinner ready, if only I hadn't said that,
but it's too late now, lying across the floor
Come back to me
Please stay away

Don't leave me alone
How much must I cry?
It's too late now, there's so much blood
Should I call the police?
Should I call a hospital?
I don't know, I don't know . . .
Go away, you who I loved so much
Leave, I say, the one you hated so
Why? Why didn't you love me?
I who adored your every touch?
S-She's still bleeding but-but she's so cold
They're all over
bloody and black welts across her flesh
shaped like my fingers, she never even told
There's darkness now and I wonder, am I dead?
That was it wasn't it? Finally killed by that man.
"He's no good for you." They all told me, everyone,
but it's too late now, I'm drowning in crimson red.
Hide her, hide her body before someone finds out
Here, beneath the porch. No one can ever know, ever.
I'm so sorry! I-I didn't mean for it to go so far, you weren't supposed to die
This wasn't supposed to happen, don't you make me cry!
Movement, harsh hands against my flesh and I want to scream
I want to run away, to flee
but it's too late now, it's too late you see
I know this now
because no one can breathe life back into me.

Stand Back
By Anonymous
16 years old

Stand back and take a step to the side
think about what you're doin', forget your stupid pride
You starin' down the silver-black barrel of a pistol

waitin' for the sound of the big man's whistle

Police are comin' down with their guns all drawn

you're standin' like a fool, your brains lost to brawn

red and blue are flashin', a stupid crime of passion

You're gonna get locked up, you ain't gettin' no compassion

Smoke risin' in the air, mixin' with grotesque pollution

I gotta admit it man, I can't think of no solution

but that don't mean you can go around town killin'

if you go down that road, there ain't no way you'll be winnin'

Little baby girl, lyin' by the roadside

blond hair blue eyes, the American home pride

walkin' home from school, didn't know what was comin'

you shot her down flat, now the girl ain't nothin'

Red, white, blue, this is what it's comin' to

blood bleaches white and justice just ain't true

we forgettin' who we are, we forgettin' we're all human

reduced to meth and murder, inside we're all fumin'

We dreamin' of "what ifs" and regrettin' "if onlys"

but if we keep on dreamin' with no actions it's gonna get lonely

we'll all end up dead, either accident or murder

just like baby girl, little Krissy Anne Shurder

Kids are lost to gangs and long lines of caine

that's what happened to you boy, can't forget the pain

when yer twelve years old and yer daddy beats ya

it's hard to stay straight but you're playin' for keeps, yeah.

But stand back and take a step to the side

think about what your doin', forget your stupid pride

It ain't over yet, not until you pull the trigger

and forget them awful words like liar and nigga

Don't make them words true, that's not the real you

you're better than this so bring back the blue

bring back justice and put away the gun

think about it man, think about your son

What's he gonna think when he sees the cops take his daddy

he ain't got no one else, he'll be alone in this world, ya see

pull the gun back, don't hurt this little girl

just because you know that you don't control your own world
Red, white, blue, this is what it's comin' to
blood bleaches white and justice just ain't true
we forgettin' who we are, we forgettin' we're all human
reduced to meth and murder, inside we're all fumin'
Just walk away man, just walk away
or it's the girl who'll have to pay
you always said that it was your own life
but now it's hers man, now it's her strife
The police are here now, they're surroundin' the scene
see you standing' with gun drawn, over little girl only thirteen
they see what's goin' on, they ain't given you a chance to attack
so with a quick bang, you get shot in the back.
Little girl gets up runnin', as you fall to the ground
there are tears in your eyes and you can't hear a sound
now you're lying on the cement, bleeding on the pavement
thinkin' 'bout your son, unable to pay rent
Blackness is your world now as you fall into your grave
and you know in your heart that it's time to be brave
you hadn't even killed nobody, yet here you are dyin'
'cause the truth is boy, that you were caught tryin'

What You Wanted
By Kail Benson
14 years old

Is this what you wanted?
They tried to reach you
You took them for granted
And did what they told you not to
Now you are locked away
You claim it wasn't your fault
But that's what you always say
Never learned the lessons taught

Your mother is devastated
To your father you never said goodbye
She says her family is dying
Disappearing before her eyes
Is this what you wanted?
To hurt everyone who loves you?
They feel so neglected
But still try to help you through
You know it's time to man up
And turn your life around
When you get the freedom you wait for
Do something to make them proud

Because He Ain't No Punk
By Anonymous
18 years old

My cousin isn't alive today
Because he ain't no punk
Some idiot blew my cousin away
Because he ain't no punk
He shot my cousin at least six times
Some people say that's asinine
And it doesn't soothe this pain of mine
When someone says, "We living in these times."
Whatever happened to what the old heads say?
You know, "It's cool to walk away."
But our generation doesn't think that way
That's why my cousin isn't here today.
Well, you love God; you say you pray.
Then let me put it this-a-way:
God shuns the haughty and raises the meek
Even Jesus turned the other cheek.
Now who am I, and who are thee

To act as if we are greater than He?
So release the hatred and stop being bitter,
Encourage your brother as respectable figures
So we can be around when our kids get bigger.
Just think about it man—'cause at this rate,
Sooner than later, we'll have no race.
Statistics limits us to age 25
Well, that means next year I won't be alive.
So I'm hoping that these words
Reach one set of ears
And they sink into his heart
So he feels what he hears.
And once I'm gone
He'll have the courage to speak up
And say, "You know, he spoke the truth
Because he ain't no punk."

R.I.P. Kascie Corie McClellan

Grace
By Alexander Banuelos
Age 21

Once in life, I met this Christian.
This little girl was on a mission;
A little bundle of ambition
And when she spoke, we loved to listen.
At her church, the most devout
Were her mother and her aunt, no doubt.
They would sway and sing, pray and shout.
Their God they could not live without.
That's what their lives were all about.
This little girl, her name was Grace.
She had freckles speckled across her face
And wore a dress with purple lace.

She read her Bible at a pace
That never once gave in to haste.
After all, it was no race.
Grace's father was never there
But it wasn't because he didn't care.
He merely thought that church impaired
His daughter's mind and wasn't fair.
And little Grace, so unaware,
Had no word in the affair.
Now, Grace's mom and dad, of course,
Were going through a rough divorce.
Every step of it was coarse
And filled her father with remorse
For such an action is a force
That carries children out of sorts.
After countless courtroom slaughters,
Grace lost her one and only father.
It could've worked, but mom didn't bother,
So dad lost custody of his daughter.
There went Grace, swept away
To go and sit in church all day—
Brainwashed, as her dad would say;
Never shown another way.
Grace was beautiful as she was bright
And as a child, had strong insight.
There were little poems she would write
And never shy, she would recite
These words that seemed to carry light
Through the darkest and most frigid nights.
With these words, she would incite
A need for the church to do what was "right."
Inspired to do something good,
They dispersed throughout the neighborhood.
Grace was told to behave as she should,
But it seemed that she misunderstood.
Convinced that God was at her side,

Grace took off at her own stride,
Knocking at each door with pride
And if anyone who did reside
Along that street did open wide,
Grace would smile and step inside.
Just down the street, outside address eighty-eight,
A thief was carrying some hefty weight.
Without finesse, thought, or debate,
He kicked straight through a rusty gate
Enclosing address eighty-eight.
The sinister robber never balked.
He kissed his loot and there it dropped.
He found a staircase, rushed to the top
And found a door that wasn't locked.
The sneaky man was hardly shocked
As he made sure his gun was cocked.
At this point, he couldn't be stopped.
And then came Grace, up the block,
Skipping along the cold sidewalk.
There stood Grace at house eighty-eight,
And though it was getting very late,
She knew that she just couldn't wait
To meet the owners of eighty-eight
With whom she'd be so enthralled to relate.
Inside the house, all the while,
The thief moved up and down an aisle,
Scowling at the dirty tile.
The house was empty—not worthwhile.
This made the burglar much more vile—
By the second, more hostile.
He headed out, but just before,
He heard a knocking at the door.
"This house is empty, so what for?"
He pondered to his conscience' core.
He had his loot, but wanted more,
So he slipped down to the first floor.

On the porch, he found Grace,
A bright expression on her face.
All he thought was, "What a waste—
An entire chunk of time debased."
Anger piled and his heart raced.
In search of blame for his distaste,
The only thing he saw was Grace.
"Little girl," he kneeled to say,
"How dare you stand here in my way.
If you plan to live another day,
Turn around and run away."
Little Grace, with her cute cunning
Told the thief she wasn't running
And that Christ, his savior, was soon coming.
The words she spoke were not so wise
For God was something he despised
And she could see it in his eyes.
It only made his anger rise.
He put the pistol to her chest
And let the bullet sort the rest.
Grace's eyes then opened wide.
If she could've, she would've cried.
Just as much as the poor girl tried,
Her body toppled to the side.
She looked up to the sky and sighed,
"Why?
You said that you would be my guide.
My mom, my church, my God . . .
They lied."
By these words, the thief, sedated,
His anger was so soon abated.
The life from little Grace was faded.
The man stood there, his soul deflated
Becoming all that now he hated.
She was dead, but there he waited
For a breath so long belated

But no life was reinstated.
It was then the man grew jaded.
"I've lived my life unsatisfied,"
The thoughtless thief then thoughtfully stated,
"Perhaps my death, too, is fated."
Spilling blood that should not have been spilt
Burdened the thief with his first flood of guilt.
It was a feeling too great for the man—
One he couldn't understand.
So he took his pistol in his hand
And sprayed his brain across the land.
Grace was a girl who should have grown
But now and always sleeps alone.
A pale face resembling stone,
A little pile of flesh and bone
Sacrificed to the unknown.
The world is cruel with God or without—
No regard to the doubtful or devout
For divinity truly has no clout
When children cry and victims shout—
When nations dry and die of drought—
When volcanoes spew from mighty spouts—
Nothing is promised until it's lights out.
Let a child live and learn.
Let their dreams soar and churn.
We've lived our lives, give them a turn.
No life can truly be enhanced
By imposing one's own spirit's stance.
Give a child—a soul—a chance.

For the River That Held Him in His Last Moments
By Taylor Johnson
19 years old

I'm sure he was not the first body to fall

into your depths
On a Sunday
when most noises are unassuming

This was not the last time your edges would become ruddy
and stain the bank red with early morning passion
You knew the break in his neck
the swell of his body
the crack in his skull

You tried to get the blood out,
I'm sure you tried to hold him
Like his mother would

A young man named Jacob Daniel was murdered in Tulsa, Oklahoma.
The following three pieces were written in response to this tragedy (Etan Thomas).

Youth Concerns
By Marco Vann
16 years old

Silent and broken
Not knowing what just happened
I lie here

Bang! Bang!
There you are lying there fighting . . .
Wanting to live, but you can barely
Handle the pain
Blood puddle
She looks at her hands
Please do not go!!
The sirens are clear
The lights flash before me
Red . . . White . . . Blue

That day feels as if it happened yesterday
It has changed me
Made me a better person
The pain still hides within me
I wish it never happened
But his spirit is watching over me

Dedication to Jacob Daniel
By Seth Amos
15 years old

You left without a goodbye, without a glance
Without a high five. You left too soon
You lived your life to the fullest
Now that you're gone I feel you are closer than before
Every time I look into the sky I remember all of the crazy times we shared and how
     much trouble we got into
Then when the night falls I look into the dark sky
I think about how you helped me through my fears
And how good of a friend you were, you are
More like a brother than a friend
Now you are part of my guardian angels along with all of my family and friends
     but to me you are a part of my family
I understand why you lived your life to the fullest
Because you never know when your time will come
I don't know you to be a hoodlum because in my eyes
You are still Jacob
Every time I hear your name it's hard to laugh at all of the funny things you did be-
     cause you are not here anymore
As I look at it, you still had a couple of more years to see
Every time I wake all I can think is that Jacob is still sleeping
He can't be dead
But he is sleeping

And always will be

Silence
By Jakkie Burten
16 years old

Silence. I get the phone call
Silence. You have been shot
Silence. I am in shock
Silence. I sit there
Silence. I am angry
Silence. Someone told me you were dead
Silence. I cried
Silence. Someone called
Silence. You are still alive
Silence. I wipe my eyes
Silence. Pull through
Silence. I love you
Silence. You fight
Silence. You try
Silence. Memories
Silence. Tears
Silence. My heart shifts gears
Silence. I smile for you
Silence. I look at your pictures
Silence. I listen to your songs
Silence. I think of you all the day long
Silence. Phone rings
Silence. You are slipping away
Silence. I'll never forget that day
Silence. Water streams from my eyes
Silence. You made it this far
Silence. But you are still too young
Silence. And too precious

Silence. Why you?
Silence. Are you dead?
Silence. Shot in your head
Silence. Please do not go
Silence. My bro
Silence. I love you so
Silence. Beep beep beeeeep
Silence. Your heart
Silence. Forever silenced
Silence. Flatline
Silence

12.
Racial Issues / Racism

*White students in my college address our 44th
President of the USA as Obama, but say Former
President Bush. And they are supposed to be educated?*
—William Thomas

Dave Zirin: Why do you think racism is so seldom discussed openly?

Etan Thomas: In this society, it's very uncomfortable for people to speak on racism or a racial issue without some catastrophic event that prompts the nationwide debate. Many want to pretend that racism doesn't exist or that we are generations removed from the racial problems of the past.

Dave Zirin: What has your experience been in speaking about the issue of racism with young people?

Etan Thomas: From my experiences, young people have no problem speaking about racism. I did notice that many still naturally segregate themselves in the school auditoriums where I am speaking. But young people do realize that racism has not gone away. From my experiences in speaking with them, I would say that they wish things were different, but are far more honest about how prevalent racism still is in present-day society than most adults are. In this chapter you will see young people explore racism and give solutions for how this country could eventually progress.

Dave Zirin: What brought you to write the poem "Confederacy" included below?

Etan Thomas: I was in Richmond, Virginia, for training camp with the Washington Wizards, and while I was down there I was in this hotel van getting something to eat, and they had to make another pickup. Well, this group of white people came in and they were talking about how their grandfather had—coincidentally—heart surgery and that the person's heart was from New York so they were teasing him about being half Yankee. I turned around and said, "What did you just say?" And she repeated it as if it was nothing major. I asked them if they still spoke in terms of the north and the

south, and they replied, "Of course. We're from Virginia. This is the capital of the Con-
federacy." They went on to tell me Robert E. Lee lived down the street from where we
were, and about how they wanted to preserve the old way of life as far as dialect, farm-
ing, and culture. I asked if they knew what the Confederate flag symbolizes. They said
it has nothing to do with slavery or racism, and I replied, "Are you serious?" I told them
that was the whole reason for the Confederacy, and that the farming was plantation
agriculture, which was slavery—and that this was the way of life that they were talking
about preserving. They kept looking at me as if they were shocked. Then my stop came
up and the conversation came to an abrupt halt. Later that evening, I wrote the poem.

The Confederacy
By Etan Thomas

I'm amazed at your ignorance
You've taken stupidity by the hand and claimed him as
your twin
Sending sensations of unenlightened kin to nestle in
locations throughout your mind
And now you're baptized in a river of foolishness for
your future generations to dance in
Never enhancing your frame of mind
Your iniquity is magnified with desires that someday
the south shall rise again
How could you aspire to return to the darkest point of
this country's past
Plastered with the pride of vicious slave masters
You haven't turned from your wicked ways
Your ancestors' days of ruling with a tyrant's raid

A malicious mind
That created our subjugated calamity
A demoralizing time
That would navigate through the circumference of our reality for centuries
A horrendous crime
Almost unforgivable if not directly ordered from above

Knowing the actions of the past
What could you possibly have to be proud of?
The old south?
I can't believe that you could possibly let that come out of your mouth
How can your idiocy last for an eternity?
That's like somebody yearning to embrace the swastika because it represents old
    Germany
Robert E. Lee, Stonewall Jackson and Jefferson Davis are the equivalents of Nazis
    to me
As evil as Kirk Lyons' Sons of Confederate Veterans party
Marching with straightened legs hailing a sign of hate
Communicating messages of evil as far as the eye can see

You want to hold on to a past of wickedness
Rain into existence the hell your forefathers created
on earth
Drenched with the blood of my people
Their tears are soaked into the essence of my history
A permanent fixture placed at the top of my past
I'm harassed with thoughts of agony
Revisited misery of a tormented soul
At the hands of a demented mind
The crime of all crimes
A four hundred year long torture chamber
Filled with whips, nooses and cries
To the tune of whistling Dixie
Their sorrow is locked like a dread within the depths of my being
Continuously seeing visions of captivity
Shackles and chains
You're disrespecting their unbearable pain
You might as well be spitting in their grave
Dancing around their tombstone while you bathe in your wicked ways
Celebrating evil
Rejoicing in the torture and persecution of my people

Their lifelong sentence

Their withered spirit
Broken like the back of a camel
Burdened with straws of weighted whips
A crippling effect
A mind left in shambles
As Willie Lynch still scrambles through our daily walks
Haunting our realities with the howling of the past
Harassing our mentalities without us even being aware

While you maintain your pride's detestable glow
Seeing your flag takes me back to the torture they had to endure
The purest form of hate
Created from a superior mind state
The audacity to enslave an entire race

Stealing me was the most wicked crime you could commit
Atrocities apparently forgotten
A rotted soul
A hidden humanity
Covered by oppression's lids
Ridding yourself free from guilt or responsibility
Let's just see if you tell the truth to your kids

"Whatchu Mixed Wit?"
By Eric Powell aka E.L.P.J. (Aswad Fahd)
15 years old

It's one of the many questions asked of a modern day adolescent,
Descendant of a people enslaved, oppressed and
Taught to hate themselves . . .
Asked usually by
Other modern day adolescents,
Descendants of a people enslaved, oppressed and
Taught to hate themselves . . .
"Whatchu Mixed Wit?"

With my dirt yellow skin color that I inherited from my mother,

Lamb wool hair, full lips and dark brown stare, I say . . .

"Nuttin', I'm Black . . . "

She tells me . . .

"Stop lyin', your hair is too 'good' for that!"

And I'm like, "Ummm . . .

I don't think hair texture should be described as 'good' or 'bad,'

Especially not when the one classified as 'bad' is the same exact one you happen to
    have . . ."

See . . . most people find this question to be harmless,

But to be honest, I find it to be the garments

That clothe self-hatred . . .

And not 'cause you mentionin' ancestors of other races,

That may be the case, it's just . . . the way you say it . . .

And ask it . . . makes it seem like you're denying your Blackness . . .

Shakin' yo' @&#es and tappin' for the masters,

Putting on a mask, thinking it's hidin' yo' madness, but . . .

You'll soon come to realize the pigment that shades in the rest of you isn't one that
    matches . . .

It's like . . .

Ali changing his name to Cassius; it's backwards,

Since we the Creator's first children and we forgotten,

Does that make us bastards?

Through the practice of a wack @%$ Christian religion,

From Catholics to Baptists, we were often cast as Satan and his minions,

While whites were depictin' themselves as Jesus, God and faithful witnesses,

The masses of slaves would go to masses on Sundays,

Where pastors told 'em being Black was a sin and

Over time this was indoctrinated into the minds of the slave children . . .

Take a mulatto child—put him in the kitchen,

Teach him that he's better 'cause he's lighter,

Now that's Willie Lynchin',

What's going on, on these plantations is experimentation,

That includes the rapin' of your foremothers, so . . .

Before you brag about your so-called "good hair" and ya light skin,

Just know, it's a slight chance that the white man's

genes is in yours 'cause he molested ya great-great grands, and . . .

And don't think you safe 'cause part of them is in you . . .

'Cause if you don't at least look a hundred percent white,

You're viewed as a n----- too . . . it's a one-drop rule . . .

So we straighten our hair, lighten our skin,

Get surgery on our nose and lips, our @$%es we bust,

Just to conform with a society that will never love us for us . . .

I taught my little sister to be proud of who she was,

That's why I pity her when she asks me,

"EJ, why are white girls prettier?"

I try to tell her that she's beautiful, and that all people are,

But I'm discouraged when I see her change her character to blonde on Poptropica.

The Westernized standard of beauty runs rampant in the movies,

Media, shows, commercials, video hoes, and all of those,

I feel a NEED . . . to break these old fallacies,

Black people . . .

What does it take to realize our kinky curly hair symbolizes spiral galaxies,

Our different shades represent different realities, and our—wait . . .

Was that too metaphysical for y'all? Uhh . . . well,

Lemme offer up some more tangible examples . . .

"Whatchu Mixed Wit?" is not a question the police ask

When they pull yo' a** over for bein' Black,

Plant on ya person crack,

Imprison you or shoot you in the back,

When you walk into that courtroom for some &#%$ you ain't do,

And you get on deathrow, and the white person who come in after you

Get 6 months, you think they knew—or rather gave a $*&%—

That you was "only half-Black"?

Old white lady hold her purse a little tighter when you walk by her?

"Why bruh? Don't she know I'm like . . . a sixteenth white? Like her?"

And I ain't a fan of no politicians,

But after seeing how them white conservative act,

Even Obama filled out on the census that he was "just Black."

Now . . .

I know, some come from a mixed heritage,

If it's a result of true love, acknowledge that,

All I'm tryna say, is never be ashamed to say . . .
That you BLACK . . .

Progress
By Jesse Ferrell
18 years old

he asked me what i was with that sly slantwise look and i started to answer:
i am . . .
but that wasn't really the question, was it?
more like:
he heard me talking on the phone as i
walked past and wanted a
one word clarification of the relationship
between my green eyes and my accent;
more like:
it seemed pale arms wrapped around his
neck might be a nice accessory, so
he approached me.

and he is?
but it doesn't really matter, does it?
since dark skin and bright sneakers
came precisely as advertised,
since it seemed brown arms wrapped around my
neck might be a nice accessory, so
i accepted.

my mother said she loves to see these
young interracial couples, that our generation

is making progress!
seems she hasn't realized that while stereotypes can polarize,
the result is sometimes a powerful magnetism.

until he really wants to know what
i am . . .
recognize the stereotypes that drew him
to me, understand that i am more than a
pale-skinned, small-breasted package of
academics and innocence,
stop making jokes about his mother,
sit through dinner forgiving the
accidental condescension of mine,
and be able to say with
honesty
that what attracts him is my style,
the way i wave my hands around when i'm
talking, or the fact that my ring-tone is Gil Scott-Heron 'cause
secretly he digs that music too . . .

and until i really want to know what he is . . .
recognize the stereotypes that drew me
to him, understand that he is more than smooth, muscled arms holding a
radio that bumps misogyny on the other side of a
rotting river, respect his sister,
stand before his grandmother without shame,
and be able to say with honesty that what attracts me are his words, the way he
picks at his roots when he's solving a problem, or the purple lines that tell
stories on the palms of his hands . . .

yeah until then,
people looking for salvation can
keep pointing to us like we're a sign of progress,
keep putting us on the cover of their
come-live-in-this-town magazines,
buy-these-fly-clothes magazines,
this-is-what-modern-looks-like magazines
but i won't be offended if y'all
tell them that's wrong.

yesterday when we were walking a
wise woman with long gray locks shook
her head at him with such sadness, and while
i don't believe that this relationship can't be, i believe
she has a point. because until i really want to know what
he is, and until he really wants to know what i am

yeah until then, y'all would be doing us a favor
if when you see people looking at us
like we're some sign of progress
you ask them,
please ask them
to look again.

Cultural Diversity
By Anonymous
17 years old

I stopped looking into myself for answers
as I grew older and
my questions still yielded more confusion
"Who am I?"
A simple three-word question
but yet when you look at brown skin with a yellow tint
and check a box marked Black
slash
African-American descent
it is larger than life
You depend on others to tell you your history
If your elder generation has committed themselves to reenergizing the earth
before you are old enough to ask that question
you can find yourself lost
taking directions from those with authority

I was told in school
during the administration of a CAT test
which box to check by teachers at the age of five
After MAT and MEAP tests,
sitting at the table with a white supremacist
who after talking guns with an eight year old stated,
"I never met such smart Negroes,"
I know what skinheads call me
and my mother's stories
of how my great-grandfather was a Native American
who changed his last name to hide his ethnicity . . .
I asked my mom,
"If I'm Native American too,
which box do I check?"
She turned to me,
"Baby, check what you feel."

When the next school board test came to check my intelligence quotient
my pen hesitated
I heard the taunts of my peers to another girl in my head
She was dark brown with short nappy hair
and told everybody she was half Indian
I remembered the look on her face
as they laughed maliciously
My pen found its course and checked the box marked "Black"
and moved to prove that more than mere quibbles filled my mind
Now, I'm grown by all stipulations of this society
But I'm still that little girl
with the same question
"Who am I?"
I envy my cousins
whose Arab father can give them a culture
where my father was absent
and void of any knowledge before his generation

I work within my own racial group

adopting bits of different cultures
I enjoy Thanksgivings
gathered around the table with
Puerto Rican friends,
Caucasian god-family from a racist family,
Arab-Muslim Americans,
Vegetarian non-denominationalists,
Christians,
Mandinkas,
and my daughter with an Ivorian father
I laugh at how the melting pot
can be shown around that very table

I can speak bits of French, Mandinka, Arabic, and Italian
curse in a couple more
I assimilate when needed
but I always come back to my own
I fight to educate our youth to discover themselves
and answer that short question through self-development
I want to contribute to this diverse society
but it seems we are segregated into different venues
so the first thing
I notice when I walk in a room is
how many black people there are
When I work with a Caucasian person
I wonder if they think we are still called Negroes
I pray that the images of hatred
birthed from ignorance
are not the image God has made us in
And for my daughter
I say another prayer:
Lord, let her father give her a culture and direction
guide people into seeing the beauty in her dark skin
accepting or hating her for herself only
Amen.

Reverse Discrimination

By Anonymous

16 years old

I didn't realize how sheltered
my world was
or in another view
segregated
This realization didn't hit me full force
until I stayed in my college dormitory

I should have been better prepared
but my high school social life
calmed some of the hurtful memories

The societal norm is that high school is hard
and filled with bullies
but for me
for the first time I was accepted

I didn't hear the jeers of peers
of how I "talked funny"
and when I cursed
"it didn't sound right"

When I wore my inherited Native beaded necklace
I didn't get called Navajo
emphasis on "jo"
Instead I met my first Native American
equipped with a tribal card

The pictures I had of white friends
were not torn up by angry black faces
while instructing me to find a friend with my own kind

My clothing's origin was not dissected
until it ended at the basement
of an interracial neighborhood church

No
these events did not happen
in the usual teenage events of high school
for they happened much earlier

I found acceptance
in my high school for gifted teenagers
so I did not notice that my white friends
were not there anymore
until the first time I walked into the eatery
on Eastern Michigan's campus

The first thing I noticed on my first survey
was that the occupants had divided into groups:
Black and all others
because any ethnicity or race other than its own
was not accepted on the "black side"
without an escort of one of its members

So when the unsuspecting Caucasian freshman
sat on the "wrong side"
he got evil stares
while conversations around him stopped

He realized his social crime
and moved to the more abundant "white side"
with "Can you believe that white boy?" trailing behind

I told the story to my sophomore roommate
and she laughed at the boy's discomfort
I looked at her
naïve as I am

She began to tell me
about my first night of dorm life

"You wrote a note that you would be back
and left your name."

I blinked at her

"You signed it Rainbow."

Another blink

"That's why I requested a room change.
I thought you were white because of your name,
and I only wanted a black roommate."

The reverse discrimination
became apparent
although I was but wasn't the intended victim
I had wondered that night
why she had a group of friends
and a bag packed to meet me

But instead of noting these acts of hostility
I offered my hand
and introduced myself

I should have pointed out the act
at the time of its conception
But naïve as I am
I,
the perceived "white girl"
did not know who or what to defend
My name?
My color,
but what is the issue?

After all her requests ended as soon
as my skin passed the color
and she left with a smile
at her new Black roommate.

We're All in This Together
By Vampirecha
19 years old

Racism. A seven letter word with a lot of meaning and history. There is no supe-
rior race in the world. There is just one race—the human race.
I'm thirteen years old and I have witnessed a lot of racism in my life. I don't un-
derstand why it matters what we look like. What matters is how we act,
our ideas, and our contribution to the world. I am friends with many peo-
ple from many races, backgrounds, and cultures.
My best friend is African American and I am Caucasian. We've been friends for
two years and nothing has changed. I am friends with a Korean young
girl from Seoul, South Korea, and she is great to talk to, and she is kind. I
am friends with Mexicans as well. I can somewhat sympathize with those
Americans who are angry with the Mexicans but they shouldn't blame
them for the bad economy—they need jobs just as much as we do.
My personal opinion is that if we set aside our differences we can focus on more
important things like terrorism, the economy, the Earth, diseases, and
most importantly—our future.
Another personal opinion of mine is that if we see the world in the eyes of young
children, we can look past our outsides and see what is on the inside.
Why? Because there is no racism in young children.
I think that we should take time to learn about other cultures and races to understand
them. And we shouldn't hold grudges. What happened in the past won't
change. We should all move on. We made mistakes but it's time to forgive.

One
By Ninlee

19 years old

Who are we to fight
When the cursed blinding hate consumes us?
It is unfortunate baring the ill-consumed thoughts that ravish the mind
Open arms and join in the true fight
The fight for
True love and unity
Blast the stereo fill it
Only with music blaring from our hearts
Hate only fuels the cycle filled with perversions of the minds
of the ones who need to open up their blinders

We need to be one
Not one by ourselves
Stop the hearsay
Pointing fingers
It is pointless

The blind leading the blind
Why do we hate?
Misjudged by our judgment
Let go of what you can't control
Embrace the separate entity we call individuality
We are different to open the mind
To educate the heart
And to strengthen each other

We need to be ONE
Not one by ourselves

Has the Dream of Dr. King Been Fulfilled?

By William Thomas

21 years old

I wasn't around when the speech was found in the mind of Dr. King,

But I am in town to pursue his dream.

I don't think we are living the dream of Dr. King despite the fact that 40 years after

　giving his speech

we have the first African American President of the USA.

The President, by the way, is a very intellectual, articulate, professional and person-

　able man,

but white America still stands to second guess his ethnicity.

His father is blacker than your shadow at night

and his mother put up every black woman's fight

in doing what she had to do for her child—the black woman's creed.

It's our fault we have not fulfilled the dream of Dr. King.

We still have brothers on the corner, mean, mugging, straight thugging,

fighting and killing each other in the streets, for nothing.

We are still disrespecting our women,

bearing the gift of semen,

but leaving fatherless homes.

We know how to put bullets in a gun but not books to our domes.

White students in my college address our 44th President of the USA as Obama,

but say Former President Bush. And they are supposed to be educated?

They are dedicated to teaching their little kids racism

by sending them to school with "NObama" shirts on.

No matter what they say,

Kanye says, "Racism is still alive. They just be concealing it."

This is what we have to deal wit.

I Am

By Christa Carter

19 years old

Standing in front of a mirror
Bright eyed and innocent
Iam saw the reflection of a stranger
The reflection of a stranger she'd always known
Little girl in a world that was not her own.

Iam was a nomad everywhere she went
No one really wanted her because she was of mixed descent.
Her mother's roots reached deep down into the earth of Africa
And her father was from the Philippines.
In love they made Iam
So she got stuck in between.
Stuck in between but left alone
Mama was an addict and daddy wouldn't dare leave mama alone
So Iam got left and they got gone.

Back to the mirror
Long kinky hair flowing over caramel skin
Iam cursed her appearance because she never fit in.
Iam wasn't black enough
"you must think you too good"
Confused because she and her persecutors grew up in the exact same hood.
And when she got around daddy's family
She never felt so black
Asking questions like "why can't I look like them?"
"why is my skin kissed by the sun?"
"why is my hair not flat?"

Weighed down was Iam by the world's stereotypes
but with the help of an elder she learned how to fight
"sticks and stones may break your bones but words will not faze you"

Iam loved her granny
Saying someday I wanna be just like you.

So Iam pressed towards the mark
Following the paths of so many others who had come before her
No longer thirsting for social acceptance because that was just tainted water
She wanted something more than anyone could give
She wanted to get know this stranger in the mirror.
Iam wanted to be free.
Free too live Iam
Free to love Iam
Free to just be Iam

The world gives us a box
And they hope we get in
But that's just not in our nature
That's not how we function as woman
We play with the cards were dealt and
We don't adapt we change our situation
Iam was a girl
Now's she's a woman
And for that there is only one explanation
In every woman there's a warrior within
We just have to connect and realize
We were never made to fit in
You can't be me and I can't be you
Be proud of who you are
And never be afraid to let your light shine true!

13.

Free Minds Book Club

Feels like you're blind
Always have to take a look behind
Sitting alone in the dark
Just seconds before your heart starts to fall apart
—Dale

Dave Zirin: What is the Free Minds Book Club?

Etan Thomas: Free Minds serves 16 and 17 year-old males who have been charged and incarcerated as adults at the DC Jail. Since 2002, Free Minds has worked with nearly 600 youths. Their mission is to introduce these young men to the life-changing power of books and writing. Some of these guys will come home soon, while others will receive lengthy sentences in federal prison. Free Minds serves them throughout their entire incarceration and is there for them when they come home. Most of the men I meet through Free Minds are going to get a second chance. The young men at the Free Minds Book Club have so much going on in their minds and in their hearts. I encourage them to write about it as a form of therapy, a way to tell their story, or to determine exactly what they want out of life. They have really opened up in an amazing way, and it is a pleasure to be able to present their words and thoughts to the world.

Dave Zirin: What is it that makes you want to work with young men in prison? What are some of the other things you try to teach them?

Etan Thomas: I have always had a passion for speaking to young men in prison. I know that many times they are not bad people, but they have just made bad decisions. I don't sugarcoat anything with them when I speak to them. I tell them of the obstacles they will surely face, how the chips are stacked against them, but that if they want to choose a different way, they can. I have seen a lot of people I grew up with go down that road, and sometimes all it takes is someone taking an interest to change their entire mind frame. A lot of times they are told that once they make a mistake, their lives are over, and I try to instill in them that many people including myself have made mistakes. But I learn from them and don't make the same mistake again.

Dave Zirin: What are you hoping to achieve through your poem "A Prison Cell"?

Etan Thomas: With this poem I wanted to show young people exactly where you can end up if you choose a life of crime. Some movies and music depict prison as if it were a cool place to be. They show it as if it isn't a living hell hole. So, I wanted to paint the picture of exactly what they could expect once they enter a prison.

A Prison Cell
by Etan Thomas

Stone walls and metal bars
A living hell on earth
Birthed through poor decisions
I'll diminish your self-worth
Make you think you're less of a man
Subhuman
Your spirit I can ruin
Insert thoughts of bringing your life to an end
You can pretend to be stronger than the son of Jerrel
Thinking you're Superman's twin
Or that you have wolverine's bones underneath your skin
But we'll see what happens when you meet me
Come in walking like you're hard I'll leave you sweeter than iced tea

When I sink my claws into your skin
You're at my mercy

Fools usually run in packs
Spinning the wheels of criminology
You're abiding by rules that don't apply once you're in captivity
Digging graves like archeology
Holding on to your gang mentality
Still set tripping

Well, go ahead
Throw it up like you're bulimic
Until you end up dead

I'll steal away the sun
The almighty one
I'll control your routine
Gladly rob you of your joy
Replace it with misery
Take hold of your freedom
And your self-esteem
You're a slave to me
Owned by correctional facilities
I tell you when to eat and sleep
You're mine

Cats rap about me
Starting wars and telling lies like their name was Dick Cheney
Strengthening their status from breathing my aroma
They think dancing with me will make their rep grow stronger
Keep dreaming
I'm steadily scheming on ways to bring you to your knees
Calculating endless possibilities
Keep praising me
I take compliments well
I've seen cats of all types
I'm the place where failed opportunities dwell
Cats that wanna roll the dice with the game of life
Trying to blame everyone but themselves

I don't know who told you that there was longevity in this drug game
How many old school gangsters do you know that are still alive
Too many Scarface movies have rotted your brain
Not even Montana and Manolo could last and survive
But you think you can do the job
Come up quick

Stack your chips
And blow up fatter than boss hog
I'm waiting for you to waive your rights for a little bit of fame
Instead of savoring the taste of sovereignty
You wanna give up your freedom for a little bit of name
From cats that you think really care about you
Like if y'all get pinched they won't snitch
And bring the boys in blue right to you
I can turn your whole crew into liars
Have them coming to your home with a wire strapped to their toe
Sell you out quicker than Sammy the Bull Gravano
So you play the corner like Cus D'amato
Nickel and dime hustling
Praying that you'll make it to see tomorrow

I watch you when you eat
Tickle your dreams while you're asleep
Massaging images of freedom to torment your fantasies
I'll have you dancing through meadows with the sun bathing your body

Breaking through the chains that held you in captivity
But you'll always wake up to me
In cold sweats from the thought of being free
I feel no remorse for your tears
Over the years I've seen plenty
Change cats to savages
After a while caged humans resemble animals

I'll take shots to your heart without splitting your skin
The end of all ends
I'll break you
You can think you're tough enough to fight me if you want to
We can go to war

I've broken down cats twice your size
I'll have you switching in high heels for the rest of your time

Lewd acts you'll be delivering
I'll hear your prayers
Even when you're whispering
Your screams will go unanswered
Ignored by COs
You'll be the key to some cat's desires
Property in exchange for protection
Fresh fish swim into the lake of fire

Y'all cats make me laugh
Tough as nails
Thinking the earth trembles when you walk
Bad as hell
Swearing that y'all can last
I'll snatch the juice right from under you
Like I'm Q on the roof holding Bishop before he is dropped to his demise

Why would you ever try to battle me?
25 with an L
Three strikes and you're out
Without the possibility of parole
And you think that you can rattle me
My style is the illest
I make cowards out of killers
I'm too much for you to handle
I die harder than Bruce Willis
Once you're with me you will never see peace
I'm as hard as they come
So welcome to the belly of the beast

Momma Don't Cry
By Antwon
18 years old

The judge left me speechless, nothing to say
I knew my Momma was gon' cry when the marshals took me away
Her pride as a mother was low, no self-esteem
When the judge stood up and said, "Title 16"
I should have known one day I'd be regretting my past
My Momma always said good things in the game don't last
Now she hurting worse than me, crying over me
If I don't call, Momma don't get no sleep
And it hurts to know she's going through all this pain
Taking her stress out on the glass and the crack cocaine
Only way I could make it better is if I change
I don't know about y'all but I'm tired of the street game
But I been doing this so long, it's all I know
I swear I be trying my best to let the fast life go
But it is calling me, calling me, and do I answer?
Momma don't cry, one day it's gon' get better
I promise

Twenty-Two
By Daniel
22 years old

I'm sittin' here on my day
The day I turn 22
Not a clue what to do
Ideas—yes very few
Listen up young dudes
This here's no lie
Was locked up six months
That's not long some might say

Now I'm home
Here on my birthday
Strugglin', livin' day to day
Today's my day and all I feel is pain
Sittin' here all alone
Not one friend I can call up on the phone
Because behind that bullet they all
Been knocked off their throne
Now they're on the way home
To see the Father most high
I'm sittin' here so selfishly askin'
Why did my father have to die?
I know I shouldn't ask why
Because everyone has their day
But today is my day
What shall this young boy do?
What's my next move?
I got a whole lot to prove
And a whole lot to make
Prayin' this day next year
I'll be able to buy myself a nice
Birthday cake

Community
By Delonte
19 years old

I'm so tired of hearing these voices on the radio
Saying the young people in the community need this
And have too much time on their hands
But when a youth asks for help
He gets off
When he seeks guidance
They're too busy

So when he gets around kids his age
Who are going through the same thing
They become the family he's been seeking all along
And no one notices what's going on
Until it's too late
And a youth is hurt or killed
They try to blame hip hop
But all I have to say about that is they need to stop!
Oprah can speak at Howard
And all that was good
But why has she never talked at Ballou or Anacostia in southeast?
Please, it's all bigger than what they say
They say they wanna help the community
But they aren't going in the communities that need the most help
Come to Barry Farms
Come to Woodland Terrace
Come to Condon Terrace
Help us!
We deserve it too
If you are wondering who is writing this
I was a lost youth
Now I'm a found young man
I lost my youth to a system that does not try to help you
Just wants to hide you in this institution or that one
And you have to struggle when you come home
To get a normal life
So I'm gonna end this for now
And ask you
What can you do to help a community?

On Display

By Kenneth

17 years old

On the train, or just in public
I receive constant stares
You'd probably think I was on display
Like the coming of a state fair
But the looks that are given aren't harmful
It's their way of saying they're scared
Or some of them just don't take the seat
Like I'm supposed to have cared
When I came into their presence
It's all eyes on me
Like I just got a major modeling deal
So many eyes on me
I think I'm in the lion's den
Getting set up for the kill
But I ain't mad at you
'Cause if I was you
I'd look at me too
I know I am put on display
But I should get paid for all the modeling I do

I Remember

By Derrick

15 years old

I remember when life was all about fun
Football, basketball . . . never about guns
I used to sit in the house and watch cartoons
Now it's so much death on the news
In everything I did, I always excelled
Now I'm stuck in this little ass cell

I wish I could take back the stupid decision I made
Sometimes when I lie down, I wish my life could fade
I have so much talent, but it's wasted on this
I sit in my cell sometimes and cry
'Cause the way I live can't be true—it has to be a lie
So much violence, need to increase the peace
I wish violence was germs, 'cause I keep some bleach
My life was hell, I wish people could see
Slavery is over, but I'm still not free
Doing wrong is easy, but doing right is hard
My mind travels to different places—I think it's on Mars
The world is falling, someone yell "Timber!"
This is just some of the stuff that I remember

Used to Be
By Gary
17 years old

I used to be that person
That would stand on the corner selling drugs
To try to keep up with the Joneses
I used to be that person
That would do anything to survive
In that jungle out there called the streets
I used to be that person
That was going to end up dead
'Cause I didn't know any better

I used to be
But now I am
That person that's willing to make a change
That person that has finally opened up his eyes
And seen that now I really have something to live for
That now I have another way out

And don't have to be
That used to be person

I used to be a boy but now I'm a man
A man with goals
And a man that plans to live
And not to ever become
That used to be person again

Internal Bleeding
By Delonte
17 years old

I cover my internal bleeding with a smile
I feel nonhuman not crying in a while
I hurt, so why won't these tears fall over?
Maybe I cried enough for a lifetime
I'm becomin' mentally strong
As I take blows from life and move on
I'd rather get over it
Than let life pass me by
'Cause life does not stop just because I cry
Sometimes I feel as if my heart and eyes
Never come in touch
Like they're beefing
And my heart says to my eyes
I'm leaving because we lost our connection
And I'm not receiving

Ghost Dad
By Juan
17 years old

Here one day and gone the next
Where did he go, my little voice vexed
Growing up without a dad, that I did
So I grew up a fatherless kid
Every three years he would call me
And every three years he told the same lie to me
He said he was going to pick me up
But he never did, so I guess he ain't give a care
Only time he really called was when he got locked up
I was always happy to talk to him, it felt like good luck
But when he finally came to see me
I thought I was dreaming
Wow! I finally saw my dad
My feelings are no longer bad
A spitting image of him, that's what I looked like
When I saw his face, I couldn't believe my sight
As soon as I closed my eyes, he was gone from under the light
I could no longer see him, I tried with all my might
Here one minute and gone the next
Where did he go, my little voice vexed
My dad, he left me, he left me to be alone
So I said forget him, I'll learn how to be grown on my own

A Cry for Help
By Juan
17 years old

Is there anybody out there
Who can help me?
These bars are taking away

243

My ability to see
They even caged up my mind
So it's no longer flying free
These bars are sealed tight
So even my mind can't break loose and flee
Even though my body is locked up
Don't mean that my brain has to be
My mind should be soaring with the eagles
Or with the fish, swimming in the sea
Someone help me please
I'm going crazy inside
It's like chess
I'm making moves that my mind couldn't decide
I'm in a place where my mind is forced to hide
And the rest of me is just in it for the ride
It's like a battle within
Easy to lose
But much more difficult to win
Someone help me please
Please hear my cry for help
Then a boy came and helped
My cry for help was felt
He was floating invisibly
Like he was stealth
And then I looked a little closer
And saw that the boy was myself
And then my mind broke through the bars
And broke through the doors
It flew in the sky with the birds and soared
My mind is now free
It ain't never coming back
It is now free to roam
And I like it like that!

Incarcerated

By Robert

18 years old

Brick walls, fences, and razor wire criss-crossed in a bind
Feelings overlooked 'cause remorse is the punishment of crime
No warmth lives here but the wind that chilled
Where it's a lot of counterfeit 'cause fake outweigh the real
Not always behind walls and locked doors while doing time
But in the outside world, incarcerated in the mind
Not always what it seems, sometimes a blessing
Only what you make of it, not always unpleasant
A learning experience that's strongly reckoned with
A chapter of one's life that'll never just shift
Forever with you, there all the way to the end
But what will you gain? Strength? Or will you bend?

Caught Up

By Kenneth

17 years old

Just a typical day in his hood
Laid back, thuggin' posted up on his block
With something to smoke and drugs to slang
He's punched in on the clock
He takes a minute surveying the strip
Making sure the coast is clear
He has a destined future, a path to pursue
But it's harder to achieve when the police are near
He still remembers what his mother said
And how his teacher compliments his work
So while he's slangin' he thinks of the opportunities beyond his ghetto dirt
"The world of big business" is how he often refers
To the place of suits and ties

And when he sees this place on TV and in magazines
He knows that's where his future lies
"But it's so far away," he thinks
A thought that clouds his mind
He's gradually slippin', abandons school
With the excuse of not having time
Now his life is moving fast
With a blurry vision of his future
And his present day events are starting to consist
Of prosecutors and a public defender as his disputer
Life ain't fun no more for him
This type of pressure is crackin' his back
He didn't even deserve the outcome
But the suits in the courtroom ain't thinking 'bout cuttin' no slack
He should've pursued his dream
Held fast to his ambition
But now he sits, waits and watches
The sordid life of prison

Inspired by Obama
By Jamal
16 years old

Today, I stand at a moment of great change and opportunity as I look out my window on the 4th of July. I realize I need to make a change and the choices I have aren't between left and right; it's my future or jail life. And I have made up my mind, it's my future. I realize I am a role model and hero to my three little sisters. So now at this defining moment in my life I am hungry for change and I find it everyone's responsibility to finally grow up and take that step forward and end with the old and start with the new. Instead of locking up our youth, let's find out what's going on and what problems we can fix. See, me, being so very intelligent, I made a lot of bad choices, not because I thought it was fun but because I had problems, physical and emotional. And I had so many questions I needed answered but had no one to talk to—no dad, brothers locked up. I've often said to myself to grow up in this world you had to be hard, but I was wrong, education will get you there in this world. So I ask myself, am I ready to take this first step in my life? Well, my answer is yes. YES I CAN!!!

Share the Pain
By Dale
17 years old

Feels like I'm in Iraq
Wakin' up every morning
Just to feel sharp pains running through my back
Feels like I'm being attacked
Feels like being here is like being at war
Wakin' up so sore
Finding yourself wakin' up every morning alone
Wishing and praying you were home
And not in this dark world alone
Feels like you're blind
Always have to take a look behind
Sitting alone in the dark
Just seconds before your heart starts to fall apart
Sitting there in the dark feeling pissed
Tempted to ball up your fist
Asking yourself, what made you decide to get into this
Fist so tight you're feeling sharp pain in the wrist
Loosening up as the tears start to come
Never regrettin' crying as the tears start to fall together
And sometimes 2 seconds apart
As I lie there in the dark

This World
By Thomas
16 years old

This world revolves around hate and crime
That happens at every drop of a dime
I feel myself curl into a ball
And think of this world as a court
Every time I make a shot
Someone dies
And my soul quivers within the walls that have formed
To block my feelings from the toxin we call hurt
But it leaks through my pores
To hurt the ones I love
Like a nightmare that haunts you at night
So I take this world one step at a time
Into the land of freedom and pride
Where this world is no more than a bitter taste
We can finally spit out
And taste the world we always hoped for
It's one thing we can imagine
But our imagination doesn't get us far
No, no, no
Not in this world

A Part of Life
By Shawn
17 years old

With my mind stuck in the gutter
I became a part of the struggle
I was always about money
So I became a part of the hustle
Get money now

And save some for later
If my pockets start hurting
Bag up soon
Sell out by noon
Dressed in all black
Call myself a young goon
Always 'bout bread
And a little bit of butter
Grew up wit' no father
All I had was a mother
Three daughters and one son
Is all she had
Put me in residential
Cause she thought I was bad
Call it tough love
And I thank her for that
How I would change my life
If I could just turn back

Elevated
By Delonte
17 years old

This generation
Money be the motivation
Wake up ready to case
With no hesitation
In these times it's MOE
And I believe I goin to be dat way
Till I die
And I love bein' fly!
Talking 'bout kicks—I'm dat guy
Young fly and flashy
That new "ish" not being fly
Irritates me like an itch

And if you told me
I had a sense for fashion
That would be an understatement
I'm all over it
Like cement on the pavement
And the older generation would
Probably tell me that's not important
I say I guess so
Look what y'all sporting
I respect Jadakiss sayin'
Why ain't brothas stackin'
Instead of bein fly
Well I'm stackin' and stay fly
Fascinated by material things
Wear jewelry to show
I'm one of the superior kings
Cause for so long America hid us in the dark
Now it's time to flood like Noah's ark
And take a stand like Rosa Parks
Moms told me when you work hard
You deserve nice things
Pops say buy the best it will last longer
So I guess you can say
It was bred in me
and now . . .

I did a big boy crime
Now I'm doin' big boy time
In the big box house
Bunkin' with dudes that got kids my age
Case manager's amazed
How I got caught up in the federal system so young
No blame, but look where I'm from
You can call it the nation's cap
But murder put us on the map
Amazed by violence

And staying out of trouble is a challenge
But nothing's worth my freedom
I got nephews and nieces
With a father that got killed by the mayhem
And with no freedom
Just wonder who's there to lead 'em
From where I'm at
Gotta get back
This ain't normal living
How I was and I am is a big difference
I think with responsibility
Doing time ain't only hurting me
And unfortunately, it hurts everyone in support of me
I let them down
But I'll generate a knockout in the next round
The haters want me to think I'm sanitation
Because of my incarceration
But somehow I elevated
And dedicated
To get money the legit way
My sentence, I thank God for that day
I know it sounds crazy
But wait and see what a man the Lord has made me
Fly

Show Me Da Way
By Gerald
17 years old

Dedicated 2 Anna Grandma

It hurts not 2 be home
It kills me 2 know you are alone
By yourself worried about me
But you always been like dat

251

Since I was three
U love me like crazy
And I know dat you do
Nothing can stop what we have
'Cause it's always been me and you
You said when I get out there
We were going 2 have a talk,
But when I get out there
I want you 2 show me how 2 walk
Walk the right road
Dat's going straight 2 the heavenly gates
Show me what must be done b4 it is 2 late
I know you're going 2 heaven
And dat's easy 2 say
I can't say dat 4 myself
But I want 2 be with you
So please
Show me da way

Moving Ahead with Excellence
By RaShawn
17 years old

Coming from a messed up background where
Boys want to let off shouts and lay strips down
Selling cocaine that is breaking my brothers and sisters down
I done had so many near death experiences
So scared of death now
I been taught as a wild child
Never to back down
To walk with a smile
Even if it should be a frown
Even when I was in school
Too busy trying to be a class clown

Having long talks with my mom
She talking about how I need to turn my life around
She praying that changes come right now
It is a shame that I had to get locked up
To find out that only I can change my life around
Moving ahead with excellence is my motivation
Every time it gets hard
I just think of that phrase
And continue my education
Thinking about when I get my high school diploma
How much paper I will be making
When I have a family
I will be bringing in all the bacon
I left bad and went good and left no traces
Going to class in jail
Working ahead, no faking
These tests are my life
Ain't no time for procrastinating
School is the way I be raking in all the information
Instead of getting paid with money
I'm getting paid with education

Change Comes
By Derrick
15 years old

Change comes when you're sick and tired
Of being sick and tired
Or when your angriness expires
But until then
You're just a jail bug stuck in a bullpen
Waiting on the judge to seal your fate
Or the marshal to lose the keys that open up the gate
Freedom, that's a lovely thing to people that don't have it

But people who do take it for granted
It's easy to say you're going to change but hard to do it
Because how can you change if you're clueless
Or maybe I'm just foolish
Could be I'm street influenced
For me there are so many changes that need to be made
That my hope for change just seems to fade
And my talents are blocked and caged
Behind a wall full of rage
Maybe if I was raised around the powerful and rich
My life wouldn't be full of could haves and ifs
Or wouldn't be blocked behind a fence
That's meant to block me away from a world full of hate
Maybe my whole meaning of being is a waste
My life is a 100% alcoholic beverage unchased
Sometimes I wonder if I was meant to be on this earth
Or maybe I was blessed with the gift or a curse
Have I changed for better or for worse?

Untitled
By DeVonte
16 years old

Part 1. Hard Times

Growing up
Mother on drugs, father in jail
Grandma got high blood pressure
All da weight's on me
Uh ruler can't even measure my pain
Be calm and stay patient
Everything uh get better
That's what they told me
Nothing changed yet
I been waiting since they told me.

Turned to the streets to find love and joy
The pain turned into anger
And I became "Rude Boy"
Young and hurt

Part 2. Torment

In the inside I'm deformed.
Out of order
Wishing I could be reborn.
This pain that follows me.
This trouble, always acknowledging me
Trying to find a way out.
But every time I look
This pain hides my escape route.
From my head to my feet
Numb me, so I can go to sleep.
My eyes are open
But I can't see
Cuz da pain is on my face blinding me.
It hurts, it stings, it's sore, it burns.
It covers my future.
It dims my light.
The pain that I receive
From living this life.

Part 3. Ready to Be a Man Now

I'm ready, I'm strong
Patiently turning grown
All da childish thoughts
All da childish acts
Like da last person, in back of da line
No more blaming others for what I did
It's time to stand and face my fears
Growing up wit no male figure

Nobody to show me what's a man's position
Now I'm woke
And my vision clear
Now I see
Being a man
Was one of my fears
Today I stand up
Head up, eyes open
Forgive me for my past
Uh new me is here at last
I'm ready to be a man

An audiobook of selections from *Voices of the Future* is available in the iTunes store and from Audible.com, including the following:

1. Intro, Nichole Thomas
2. Thankful
3. I Can't Wait To See You
4. Interlude, Malcolm Thomas
5. Bob Marley, featuring Julian Thomas
6. Voting
7. Interlude, Malcolm Thomas
8. Inauguration, featuring Fred Bodger (Etan and Julian Thomas' grandfather)
9. It's Time For A Change, Julian Thomas' Interpretation
10. Scare Tactics, featuring Julian Thomas
11. Don't Talk To Me About Love, Julian Thomas
12. Jessica Care Moore (Medusa)
13. Interlude, Nichole Thomas
14. Haters, Part 2
15. Interlude, Nichole Thomas
16. The Trap
17. A Prison Cell
18. Through with Religion
19. Negatively Influenced, featuring Julian Thomas
20. AIDS
21. It's Time for a Change, Etan's Interpretation
22. Pigs
23. My Brothas
24. Outro, Baby Imani

CD produced by Rocky Bright.
Mixed and mastered by El Rico "Ghost" Gillison.

About the Author

Etan Thomas is *More Than an Athlete*. Thomas defies the stereotype of the apoliti-cal athlete and plants his roots in a literary career that takes on controversial topics, such as the death penalty, the GOP, and racism.

This young, fiery poet approaches his work fearlessly. He has been described by Hall of Famer Kareem Abdul Jabbar as "the poetic voice of his generation" and by hip-hop legend Chuck D of Public Enemy as "a portal of our future." Thomas re-ceived the 2010 National Basketball Players Association Community Contribution Award as well as the 2009 Dr. Martin Luther King Jr. Foundation Legacy Award. His work includes serving as a surrogate for Barack Obama '08 presidential campaign and a guest speaker with DNC chair Governor Howard Dean during the "Register for Change" 50 state bus tour.

In 2005, Thomas released a collection of poems called *More Than an Athlete*. In May 2012 he released his second book, called *Fatherhood (Rising to the Ultimate Chal-lenge)*, and started a Fatherhood Movement in which he goes from city to city holding panels and town hall meetings to discuss fatherhood. In each city he recruits different celebrities to join him in inspiring an entire generation. He takes his message to pris-ons, universities, churches, high schools, and various conventions, including the NAACP convention and the Congressional Black Caucus. His writings have appeared in CNN, ESPN, the *Washington Post, Huffington Post, Hoopshype.com*, and *Slamonline*.